by Adrienne Rich

Midnight Salvage: Poems 1995–1998

Dark Fields of the Republic: Poems 1991–1995

What Is Found There: Notebooks on Poetry and Politics

Collected Early Poems 1950–1970

An Atlas of the Difficult World: Poems 1988–1991

Time's Power: Poems 1985–1988

Blood, Bread, and Poetry: Selected Prose 1979–1986

Your Native Land, Your Life

The Fact of a Doorframe: Poems Selected and New 1950–1984

Sources

A Wild Patience Has Taken Me This Far

On Lies, Secrets, and Silence: Selected Prose 1966–1978

The Dream of a Common Language

Twenty-one Love Poems

Of Woman Born: Motherhood as Experience and Institution

Poems: Selected and New, 1950–1974

Diving into the Wreck

The Will to Change

Leaflets

Necessities of Life

Snapshots of a Daughter-in-Law

The Diamond Cutters

A Change of World

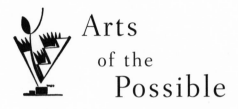

Arts
of the
Possible

W. W. Norton & Company

NEW YORK · LONDON

Arts
of the
Possible

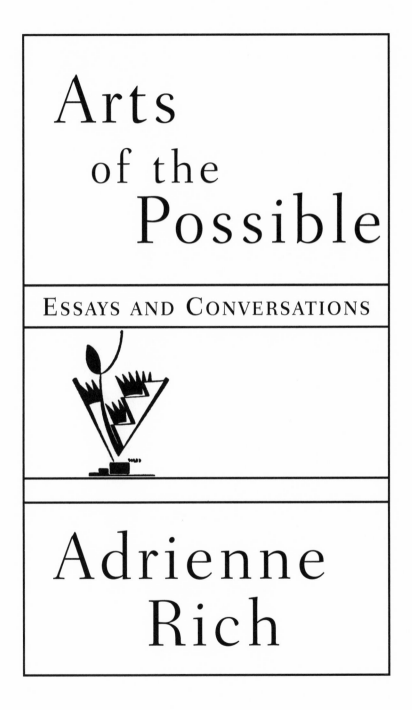

Adrienne
Rich

For information about permission to reproduce selections from this book,
write to Permissions, W. W. Norton & Company, Inc., 500 Fifth Avenue,
New York, NY 10110

The text of this book is composed in Fairfield Medium
with the display set in Fairfield Light.
Composition by Allentown Digital Services Division of
R. R. Donnelley & Sons Company.
Manufacturing by Haddon Craftsmen, Inc.
Book design by Antonina Krass.
Stenciled book ornament by William Addison Dwiggins.

Library of Congress Cataloging-in-Publication Data
Rich, Adrienne Cecile.
    Arts of the possible: essays and conversations/Adrienne Rich.
        p.   cm.
    Includes index.
    ISBN 0-393-05045-9
    1. Rich, Adrienne Cecile—Interviews.   2. Poets, American—
20th century—Interviews.   3. Poetry—Authorship.   4. Poetry.   I. Title.
PS3535.I233 A83 2001
811'.54—dc21
[B]   00-051522

W. W. Norton & Company, Inc., 500 Fifth Avenue, New York, NY 10110
www.wwnorton.com

W. W. Norton & Company, Ltd., 10 Coptic Street, London WC1A 1PU

1 2 3 4 5 6 7 8 9 0

Contents

Foreword ✕ 1

"When We Dead Awaken": Writing as Re-Vision ✕ 10
Women and Honor: Some Notes on Lying ✕ 30
Blood, Bread, and Poetry: The Location of
the Poet ✕ 41

Notes toward a Politics of Location ✕ 62
Raya Dunayevskaya's Marx ✕ 83
Why I Refused the National Medal for the Arts ✕ 98
Defying the Space That Separates ✕ 106
Poetry and the Public Sphere ✕ 115
Muriel Rukeyser: Her Vision ✕ 120
Some Questions from the Profession ✕ 128
Interview with Rachel Spence ✕ 138
Arts of the Possible ✕ 146

Notes ✕ 169
Acknowledgments ✕ 177
Index ✕ 179

For my grandchildren
Julia and Charlie

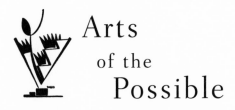

Arts
of the
Possible

Foreword

For some readers, the first four essays in this volume may seem to belong to a bygone era. I include them here as background, indicating certain directions in my thinking both about poetry and about the society in which I was writing twenty to thirty years ago. A burgeoning women's movement in the 1970s and early 1980s incited and provided the occasions for them, created their ecology. But, as I suggested in "Notes toward a Politics of Location," my thinking was unable to fulfill itself within feminism alone.

Our senses are currently whip-driven by a feverish new pace of technological change. The activities that mark us as human, though, don't begin, exist in, or end by such a calculus. They pulse, fade out, and pulse again in human tissue, human nerves, and in the elemental humus of memory, dreams, and art, where there are no bygone eras. They are in us, they can speak to us, they can teach us if we desire it.

In fact, for Westerners to look back on 1900 is to come full face upon ourselves in 2000, still trying to grapple with the hectic power of capitalism and technology, the displacement of the social will into the accumulation of money and things. "Thus" (Karl Marx in 1844) "all physical and intellectual senses [are] replaced by the simple alienation of all these senses, the sense of having." We have been here all along.

In selecting a few essays from my earlier work for this collection, I sometimes had a rueful sense of how one period's necessary strategies can mutate into the monsters of a later time. The accurate feminist perceptions that women's lives, historically or individually, were mostly unrecorded and that *the personal is political* are cases in point. Feminism has depended heavily on the concrete testimony of individual women, a testimony that was meant to accumulate toward *collective* understanding and practice. In "When We Dead Awaken," I borrowed my title from Ibsen's last play, written in 1900. Certainly the issues Ibsen had dramatized were very much alive. I "used myself" to illustrate a woman writer's journey, rather tentatively. In 1971 this still seemed a questionable, even illegitimate, approach, especially in a paper to be given at an academic convention.

Soon thereafter, personal narrative was becoming valued as the true coin of feminist expression. At the same time, in every zone of public life, personal and private solutions were being marketed by a profit-driven corporate system, while collective action and even collective realities were mocked at best and at worst rendered historically sterile.

By the late 1990s, in mainstream American public discourse, personal anecdote was replacing critical argument, true confessions were foregrounding the discussion of ideas. A feminism that sought to engage race and colonialism, the global monoculture of United States corporate and military interests, the specific locations and agencies of women within all this was being countered by the marketing of a United States model of female—or feminine—self-involvement and self-improvement, devoid of political context or content.

Still, those four early essays suggest the terrain where I started: a time of imaginative and intellectual ferment, when many kinds of transformations seemed possible. "Women and Honor" belongs to a period when there was in the air a theoretical code of ethical responsibility among women: a precarious solidarity of gender. Within that ethic—which I shared—I was trying to criticize the deceptions we practiced on each other and ourselves. Published at a time of vigorous feminist small-press pamphleteering, "Women and Honor" seemed, for a while, *usable*. Today, the parts that most interest me are the descriptions of how lying can disrupt the internal balance of the one who accepts the lie, and the difficulties of constructing an honorable life. I believe these stretch beyond gender to other hoped-for pacts, comradeships, and conversations, including those between the citizen and her government. (I do not believe that truth-telling exists in a bubble, sealed off from the desire for justice.)

Looking back on her own earlier writings, Susan Sontag has remarked: "Now the very idea of the serious (and the honorable) seems quaint, 'unrealistic,' to most people." Like other serious and vibrant movements, feminism was to be countered by cultural patterns unforeseen before the 1980s: a growing middle-class self-absorption and indifference both to ideas and to the larger social order, along with the compression of media power and resources into fewer and fewer hands, during and beyond the Reagan years.

It interests me that in "Women and Honor," that poetically terse piece of writing, I first invoked the name of Marx—to dismiss Marxism "for women." I was of course echoing the standard anti-Marxism of the postwar American cultural and political mainstream. But, as I indicate in "Raya Dunayevskaya's Marx"—written more than a decade later— this anti-Marxism, uncriticized and uninvestigated, was present also in the women's movement. Marxism was tainted there, both by garden-variety anticommunism and by the fear that class would erase gender once again, when gender was just beginning to be understood as a political category.

Sometime around 1980 I felt impelled to go back and read what I had dismissed or felt threatened by: I had to find out what Marx, along the way of his own development, had actually *written.* I began working my way through those writings, in the assorted translations and editions available to me, an autodidact and an outsider, not an academic or post-Marx Marxist. There were passages that whetted my hunger; others I traversed laboriously and in intellectual fatigue. I understood that I was sometimes overhearing early nineteenth-century German philosophical diatribes I could just as well skip.

What kept me going was the sense of being in the company of a great geographer of the human condition; and, specifically, a sense of *recognition:* how profit-driven economic relations filter into zones of thought and feeling. Marx's depiction of early nineteenth-century capitalism and its dehumanizing effect on the social landscape rang truer than ever at the century's end.

Along with that flare of recognition came profound respect and empathy for Marx's restless vision of human capacities and the nature of their frustration. I found no blueprint for a future utopia, but a skilled diagnosis of skewed and disfigured human relationships. I found a Marx who would have been revolted by Stalinism, by the expropriation of his ideas in the name of tyranny, by the expropriation of his name: "I am not a marxist," he said.

In the feminism I had embraced, as in the social field where it was rooted, there was a salient dialectic: racism as destructive presence, race as great social teacher. Time and again racial actualities pushed against the "primary oppression" of gender; time and again the lesson was forgotten. I came to realize that we were afraid: that a focus on class (read Marxism) might blot out a focus on gender and race; that gender (feminism) might blot out race and class; that you could look at history and see the big eraser wiping out each successive lesson of justice, so that collective knowledge could not accumulate. For the pressing motif of this excessive society was and is: *There is not enough (space, livelihood, validation) for all.*

I'm not sure that I could have read Marx with so much patience and appetite had I not participated in the inevitable shortcomings of the feminist movement in the United States. Though some feminists (mostly women of color) insisted on intersections of race, class, and gender, emphasis was more often laid on women's individual class identifications and how they negotiated them, or on poverty and welfare, than on how class, poverty, and the need for welfare are produced and perpetuated in the first place. (Both kinds of work, of course, are necessary.) Elsewhere, *movement* was being parochialized into "women's culture." Meanwhile, the expansion of capitalism's force field, the impoverishment of women within it, and the steep concentration of wealth were all brutally accelerating.

We can think of second-wave feminism as a splinter off the radical movements of U.S. history, especially the Depression-driven movements of the 1930s and 1940s, movements always under fire, repressed in the 1950s, resurgent in new forms in the 1960s, and, by the 1970s, again being deliberately defused and isolated. Above all, the political groupings of African Americans were under hostile surveillance. Earlier,

Malcolm X and Martin Luther King, Jr.—both leaders with large constituencies—had been murdered just as each was unscrolling a map on which race and class intersected in a shared landscape. The blotting of those maps was accomplished by violence, persecution, censorship, and propaganda. The energy, hopefulness, brains, and passion of a women's movement erupting in the United States at such a time was no match for these political circumstances. The important legacies of that movement reside not in the names of a few women starring in the media, but in the many lifesaving, stubbornly ongoing grassroots organizations it had the power to ignite. I still believe what I wrote in 1971: *A change in the concept of sexual identity is essential if we are not to see the old political order reassert itself in every new revolution.*

What prose I wrote in the 1990s was fired by a hope of bringing together ideas that had been forcibly severed from each other or thrown into competition: such as the making of literature and public education. Sometimes I felt ideas that attracted me mutually repelling each other. Or I felt the shortcomings of my own language pitted against a lethargic liberalism or a despicable rhetoric of "spin." Sometimes it all seemed mere Sisyphean effort, pushing uphill and futureless a rock bearing sweaty handprints of so many others.

But Sisyphus is not, finally, a useful image. You don't roll some unitary boulder of language or justice uphill; you try with others to assist in cutting and laying many stones, designing a foundation. One of the stonecutter-architects I met was Muriel Rukeyser, whose work I had begun reading in depth in the 1980s. Through her prose Rukeyser had engaged me intellectually; her poetry, however, in its range and daring, held me first and last. "Her Vision" is a tribute to the mentorship of her work. Another was Raya Dunayevskaya, who wrote vividly and trenchantly of the concrete revolutionary lives of women, and whose fusion of Marx's humanism with contemporary feminisms expanded my sense of the possibilities of both.

I was also undertaking a kind of research into poetics, both as writing and as reading. I had always worked fairly instinctually and independently as a poet, distrusting groups and manifestos, which I found mostly unuseful in their exclusionary male compadreship; I trusted their poetry more than their bondings. (I have had to reckon in and out of gender to do my work.) But it seemed to me that an accumulating incoherence and disruption of public language and images in the late twentieth century was something poets had to reckon with, not just for our own work. I had explored this challenge in my 1993 book, *What Is Found There: Notebooks on Poetry and Politics.* I was looking for poetics and practice that could resist degraded media and a mass entertainment culture, both of them much more pervasive and powerful than earlier in the century.

There was nothing new about this; artists have long made art against the commodity culture. And innovative or transgressive art has itself been commodified, yet has dialectically frictioned new forms and imaginings into existence.

One of the questions that pursued me is whether, and how, innovative or so-called avant-garde poetics are necessarily or even potentially revolutionary: Do they simply embrace a language so deracinated that it is privy in its rebellions only to a few? The question is not unreasonable given the decidedly antibourgeois, anticonformist claims of avant-garde tradition. The obverse question is inescapable: Must a radical social imagination clothe itself in a language worn thin by usage or debased by marketing, promotion, and the will to power? In order to meet that will to power, must we choose between the nonreferential and the paraphrasable?

I believe in the necessity for a poetic language untethered

from the compromised language of state and media. Yet how, I have wondered, can poetry persist as a ligatory art rather than as an echo chamber of fragmentation and alienation? Can the language of poetry become too abstract (some might say elitist) even as it tries to claim what Octavio Paz has called "the other voice"? Is there a way of writing on the edge? Of course I think there is, and has been; I test my own work from that likelihood. "Language," I find in Marx, "is the presence of the community." In a 1979 essay by Gary Snyder: "The community and its poetry are not two."

Are writers, poets, artists, thinking people still merely gnashing away at the problems of the early twentieth century? But this is not "mere." These primal, unsilenced questions pursue us, wherever we are trying to live conscientiously in the time we have. A new century, even a new technology, doesn't of itself produce newness. It is live human beings, looking in all directions, who will do this.

For more than fifty years I have been writing, tearing up, revising poems, studying poets from every culture and century available to me. I have been a poet of the oppositional imagination, meaning that I don't think my only argument is with myself. This book is for people who want to imagine and claim wider horizons and carry on about them into the night, rather than rehearse the landlocked details of personal quandaries or the price for which the house next door just sold.

At times in the past decade and a half I have felt like a stranger in my own country. I seem not to speak the official language. I believe many others feel like this, not just as poets or intellectuals but as citizens—accountable yet excluded from power. I began as an American optimist, albeit a critical one, formed by our racial legacy and by the Vietnam War. In both these cases it was necessary to look hard truths in the face in order to change horrible realities. I believed, with many others, that my country's historical aquifers were flowing in that direction of democratic change. I became an American skeptic, not as to the long search for justice and dignity, which is part of all human history, but in the light of my nation's leading role in demoralizing and destabilizing that search, here at home and around the world. Perhaps just such a passionate skepticism, neither cynical nor nihilistic, is the ground for continuing.

Adrienne Rich
June 2000

"When We Dead Awaken":
Writing as Re-Vision

This talk was written for a forum on "The Woman Writer in the Twentieth Century," presented in Chicago, December 1971, by the Modern Language Association's Commission on the Status of Women in the Profession. It was published in College English 34, *no. 1 (1972), and in* American Poets in 1976, *edited by William Heyen (New York: Bobbs-Merrill, 1976).*

Ibsen's *When We Dead Awaken* is a play about the use that the male artist and thinker—in the process of creating culture as we know it—has made of women, in his life and in his work; and about a woman's slow, struggling awakening to the use to which her life has been put. Bernard Shaw wrote in 1900 of this play:

> **[Ibsen] shows us that no degradation ever devized or permit-
> ted is as disastrous as this degradation; that through it
> women can die into luxuries for men and yet can kill them;
> that men and women are becoming conscious of this; and
> that what remains to be seen as perhaps the most interesting
> of all imminent social developments is what will happen
> "when we dead awaken."**

It's exhilarating to be alive in a time of awakening consciousness; it can also be confusing, disorienting, and painful. This awakening of dead or sleeping consciousness has already affected the lives of millions of women, even those who don't know it yet. It is also affecting the lives of men, even those who deny its claims upon them. The argument will go on whether an oppressive economic class system is responsible for the oppressive nature of male/female relations, or whether, in fact, patriarchy—the domination of the fathers—is the original model of oppression on which all others are based. But in the last few years the women's movement has drawn inescapable and illuminating connections between our sexual lives and our political institutions. The sleepwalkers are coming awake, and for the first time this awakening has a collective reality; it is no longer such a lonely thing to open one's eyes.

Re-vision—the act of looking back, of seeing with fresh eyes, of entering an old text from a new critical direction—is for women more than a chapter in cultural history: it is an act of survival. Until we can understand the assumptions in which we are drenched we cannot know ourselves. And this drive to self-knowledge, for women, is more than a search for identity: it is part of our refusal of the self-destructiveness of male-dominated society. A radical critique of literature, feminist in its impulse, would take the work first of all as a clue to how we live, how we have been living, how we have been led to imagine ourselves, how our language has trapped as well as liberated us, how the very act of naming has been till now a male prerogative, and how we can begin to see and name—and therefore live—afresh. A change in the concept of sexual identity is essential if we are not going to see the old political order reassert itself in every new revolution. We need to know the writing of the past, and know it differently than we have ever known it; not to pass on a tradition but to break its hold over us.

For writers, and at this moment for women writers in particular, there is the challenge and promise of a whole new psychic geography to be explored. But there is also a difficult and dangerous walking on the ice, as we try to find language and images for a consciousness we are just coming into, and with little in the past to support us. I want to talk about some aspects of this difficulty and this danger.

Jane Harrison, the great classical anthropologist, wrote in 1914 in a letter to her friend Gilbert Murray:

> **By the by, about "Women," it has bothered me often—why do women never want to write poetry about Man as a sex—why is Woman a dream and a terror to man and not the other way around? . . . Is it mere convention and propriety, or something deeper?**

I think Jane Harrison's question cuts deep into the myth-making tradition, the romantic tradition; deep into what women and men have been to each other; and deep into the psyche of the woman writer. Thinking about that question, I began thinking of the work of two twentieth-century women poets, Sylvia Plath and Diane Wakoski. It strikes me that in the work of both Man appears as, if not a dream, a fascination and a terror; and that the source of the fascination and the terror is, simply, Man's power—to dominate, tyrannize, choose, or reject the woman. The charisma of Man seems to come purely from his power over her and his control of the world by force, not from anything fertile or life-giving in him. And, in the work of both these poets, it is finally the woman's sense of *herself*—embattled, possessed—that gives the poetry its dynamic charge, its rhythms of struggle, need, will, and female energy. Until recently this female anger and this furious awareness of the Man's power over her were not available materials to the female poet, who tended to write of Love as the source of her suffering, and to view that victimization by Love as an almost inevitable fate. Or, like Marianne Moore and Elizabeth Bishop, she kept sexuality at a measured and chiseled distance in her poems.

One answer to Jane Harrison's question has to be that historically men and women have played very different parts in each others' lives. Where woman has been a luxury for man, and has served as the painter's model and the poet's muse, but also as comforter, nurse, cook, bearer of his seed, secretarial assistant, and copyist of manuscripts, man has played a quite different role for the female artist. Henry James repeats an incident which the writer Prosper Mérimée described, of how, while he was living with George Sand,

> **he once opened his eyes, in the raw winter dawn, to see his companion, in a dressing-gown, on her knees before the domestic hearth, a candlestick beside her and a red *madras* round her head, making bravely, with her own hands the fire that was to enable her to sit down betimes to urgent pen and paper. The story represents him as having felt that the spectacle chilled his ardor and tried his taste; her appearance was unfortunate, her occupation an inconsequence, and her industry a reproof—the result of all which was a lively irritation and an early rupture.**

The specter of this kind of male judgment, along with the misnaming and thwarting of her needs by a culture controlled by males, has created problems for the woman writer: problems of contact with herself, problems of language and style, problems of energy and survival.

In rereading Virginia Woolf's *A Room of One's Own* (1929) for the first time in some years, I was astonished at the sense of effort, of pains taken, of dogged tentativeness, in the tone of that essay. And I recognized that tone. I had heard it often enough, in myself and in other women. It is the tone of a woman determined not to appear angry, who is *willing* herself to be calm, detached, and even charming in a roomful of men where things have been said which are attacks on her very integrity. Virginia Woolf is addressing an audience of women, but she is acutely conscious—as she always was—of being overheard by men: by Morgan and Lytton and Maynard Keynes and for that matter by her father, Leslie Stephen. She drew the language out into an exacerbated thread in her determination to have her own sensibility yet protect it from those masculine presences. Only at rare moments in that essay do you hear the passion in her voice; she was trying to sound as cool as Jane Austen, as Olympian as Shakespeare, because that is the way the men of the culture thought a writer should sound.

No male writer has written primarily or even largely for women, or with the sense of women's criticism as a consideration when he chooses his materials, his theme, his language. But to a lesser or greater extent, every woman writer has written for men even when, like Virginia Woolf, she was supposed to be addressing women. If we have come to the point when this balance might begin to change, when women can stop being haunted, not only by "convention and propriety" but by internalized fears of being and saying themselves, then it is an extraordinary moment for the woman writer—and reader.

I have hesitated to do what I am going to do now, which is to use myself as an illustration. For one thing, it's a lot easier and less dangerous to talk about other women writers. But there is something else. Like Virginia Woolf, I am aware of the women who are not with us here because they are washing the dishes and looking after the children. Nearly fifty years after she spoke, that fact remains largely unchanged. And I am thinking also of women whom she left out of the picture altogether—women who are washing other people's dishes and caring for other people's children, not to mention women who went on the streets last night in order to feed their children. We seem to be special women here, we have liked to think of ourselves as special, and we have known that men would tolerate, even romanticize us as special, as long as our words and actions didn't threaten their privilege of tolerating or rejecting us and our work according to *their* ideas of what a special woman ought to be. An important insight of the radical women's movement has been how divisive and how ultimately destructive is this myth of the special woman, who is also the token woman. Every one of us here in this room has had great luck—we are teachers, writers, academicians; our own gifts could not have been enough, for we all know women whose gifts are buried or aborted. Our struggles can have meaning and our privileges—however precarious under patriarchy—can be justified only if they can help to change the lives of women whose gifts—and whose very being—continue to be thwarted and silenced.

My own luck was being born white and middle-class into a house full of books, with a father who encouraged me to read and write. So for about twenty years I wrote for a particular man, who criticized and praised me and made me feel I was indeed "special." The obverse of this, of course, was that I tried for a long time to please him, or rather, not to displease him. And then of course there were other men—writers, teachers—the Man, who was not a terror or a dream but a literary master and a master in other ways less easy to acknowledge. And there were all those poems about women, written by men: it seemed to be a given that men wrote poems and women frequently inhabited them. These women were almost always beautiful, but threatened with the loss of beauty, the loss of youth—the fate worse than death. Or, they were beautiful and died young, like Lucy and Lenore. Or, the woman was like Maud Gonne, cruel and disastrously mistaken, and the poem reproached her because she had refused to become a luxury for the poet.

A lot is being said today about the influence that the myths and images of women have on all of us who are products of culture. I think it has been a peculiar confusion to the girl or woman who tries to write because she is peculiarly susceptible to language. She goes to poetry or fiction looking for *her* way of being in the world, since she too has been putting words and images together; she is looking eagerly for guides, maps, possibilities; and over and over in the "words' masculine persuasive force" of literature she comes up against something that negates everything she is about: she meets the image of Woman in books written by men. She finds a terror and a dream, she finds a beautiful pale face, she finds La Belle Dame Sans Merci, she finds Juliet or Tess or Salomé, but precisely what she does not find is that absorbed, drudging, puzzled, sometimes inspired creature, herself, who sits at a desk trying to put words together.

So what does she do? What did I do? I read the older women poets with their peculiar keenness and ambivalence: Sappho, Christina Rossetti, Emily Dickinson, Elinor Wylie, Edna Millay, H. D. I discovered that the woman poet most admired at the time (by men) was Marianne Moore, who was maidenly, elegant, intellectual, discreet. But even in reading these women I was looking in them for the same things I had found in the poetry of men, because I wanted women poets to be the equals of men, and to be equal was still confused with sounding the same.

I know that my style was formed first by male poets: by the

men I was reading as an undergraduate—Frost, Dylan Thomas, Donne, Auden, MacNiece, Stevens, Yeats. What I chiefly learned from them was craft. But poems are like dreams: in them you put what you don't know you know. Looking back at poems I wrote before I was twenty-one, I'm startled because beneath the conscious craft are glimpses of the split I even then experienced between the girl who wrote poems, who defined herself in writing poems, and the girl who was to define herself by her relationships with men. "Aunt Jennifer's Tigers" (1951), written while I was a student, looks with deliberate detachment at this split.

> Aunt Jennifer's tigers stride across a screen,
> Bright topaz denizens of a world of green.
> They do not fear the men beneath the tree;
> They pace in sleek chivalric certainty.
>
> Aunt Jennifer's fingers fluttering through her wool
> Find even the ivory needle hard to pull.
> The massive weight of Uncle's wedding band
> Sits heavily upon Aunt Jennifer's hand.
>
> When Aunt is dead, her terrified hands will lie
> Still ringed with ordeals she was mastered by.
> The tigers in the panel that she made
> Will go on striding, proud and unafraid.

In writing this poem, composed and apparently cool as it is, I thought I was creating a portrait of an imaginary woman. But this woman suffers from the opposition of her imagination, worked out in tapestry, and her life-style, "ringed with ordeals she was mastered by." It was important to me that Aunt Jennifer was a person as distinct from myself as possible—distanced by the formalism of the poem, by its objective, observant tone—even by putting the woman in a different generation.

In those years formalism was part of the strategy—like asbestos gloves, it allowed me to handle materials I couldn't pick up bare-handed. A later strategy was to use the persona of a man, as I did in "The Loser" (1958):

A man thinks of the woman he once loved: first, after her wedding, and then nearly a decade later.

I
I kissed you, bride and lost, and went
home from that bourgeois sacrament,
your cheek still tasting cold upon
my lips that gave you benison
with all the swagger that they knew—
as losers somehow learn to do.

Your wedding made my eyes ache; soon
the world would be worse off for one
more golden apple dropped to ground
without the least protesting sound,
and you would windfall lie, and we
forget your shimmer on the tree.

Beauty is always wasted: if
not Mignon's song sung to the deaf,
at all events to the unmoved.
A face like yours cannot be loved
long or seriously enough.
Almost, we seem to hold it off.

II
Well, you are tougher than I thought.
Now when the wash with ice hangs taut
this morning of St. Valentine,

I see you strip the squeaking line,
your body weighed against the load,
and all my groans can do no good.

Because you are still beautiful,
though squared and stiffened by the pull
of what nine windy years have done.
You have three daughters, lost a son.
I see all your intelligence
flung into that unwearied stance.

My envy is of no avail.
I turn my head and wish him well
who chafed your beauty into use
and lives forever in a house
lit by the friction of your mind.
You stagger in against the wind.

I finished college, published my first book by a fluke, it seemed to me, and broke off a love affair. I took a job, lived alone, went on writing, fell in love. I was young, full of energy, and the book seemed to mean that others agreed I was a poet. Because I was also determined to prove that as a woman poet I could also have what was then defined as a "full" woman's life, I plunged in my early twenties into marriage and had three children before I was thirty. There was nothing overt in the environment to warn me: these were the fifties, and in reaction to the earlier wave of feminism, middle-class women were making careers of domestic perfection, working to send their husbands through professional schools, then retiring to raise large families. People were moving out to the suburbs, technology was going to be the answer to everything, even sex; the family was in its glory. Life was extremely private; women were isolated from each other by the loyalties of marriage. I have a sense that women didn't talk to each other much in the fifties—not about their secret emptinesses, their frustrations. I went on trying to write; my second book and first child appeared in the same month. But by the time that book came out I was already dissatisfied with those poems, which seemed to me mere exercises for poems I hadn't written. The book was praised, however, for its "gracefulness"; I had a marriage and a child. If there were doubts, if there were periods of null depression or active despairing, these could only mean that I was ungrateful, insatiable, perhaps a monster.

About the time my third child was born, I felt that I had either to consider myself a failed woman and a failed poet, or to try to find some synthesis by which to understand what was happening to me. What frightened me most was the sense of drift, of being pulled along on a current which called itself my destiny, but in which I seemed to be losing touch with whoever I had been, with the girl who had experienced her own will and energy almost ecstatically at times, walking around a city or riding a train at night or typing in a student room. In a poem about my grandmother I wrote (of myself): "A young girl, thought sleeping, is certified dead" ("Halfway"). I was writing very little, partly from fatigue, that female fatigue of suppressed anger and loss of contact with my own being; partly from the discontinuity of female life with its attention to small chores, errands, work that others constantly undo, small children's constant needs. What I did write was unconvincing to me; my anger and frustration were hard to acknowledge in or out of poems because in fact I cared a great deal about my husband and my children. Trying to look back and understand that time I have tried to analyze the real nature of the conflict. Most, if not all, human lives are full of fantasy—passive day-dreaming which need not be acted on. But to write poetry or fiction, or even to think well, is not to fantasize, or to put fantasies on paper. For a poem to coalesce, for a character or an action to take shape, there has to be an imaginative transformation of reality which is in no way passive. And a certain freedom of the mind is needed—freedom to press on, to enter the currents of your thought like a glider pilot, knowing that your motion can be sustained, that the buoyancy of your attention will not be suddenly snatched away. Moreover, if the imagination is to transcend and transform experience it has to question, to challenge, to conceive of alternatives, perhaps to the very life you are living at that moment. You have to be free to play around with the notion that day might be night, love might be hate; nothing can be too sacred for the imagination to turn into its opposite or to call experimentally by another name. For writing is re-naming. Now, to be maternally with small children all day in the old way, to be with a man in the old way of marriage, requires a holding-back, a putting-aside of that imaginative activity, and demands instead a kind of conservatism. I want to make it clear that I am *not* saying that in order to write well, or think well, it is necessary to become unavailable to others, or to become a devouring ego. This has been the myth of the masculine artist and thinker; and I do not accept it. But to be a female human being trying to fulfill traditional female functions in a traditional way *is* in direct conflict with the subversive function of the imagination. The word *traditional* is important here. There must be ways, and we will be finding out more and more about them, in which the energy of creation and the energy of relation can be united. But in those years I always felt the conflict as a failure of love in myself. I had thought I was choosing a full life: the life available to most men, in which sexuality, work, and parenthood could coexist. But I felt, at twenty-nine, guilt toward the people closest to me, and guilty toward my own being.

I wanted, then, more than anything, the one thing of which

there was never enough: time to think, time to write. The fifties and early sixties were years of rapid revelations: the sit-ins and marches in the South, the Bay of Pigs, the early antiwar movement, raised large questions—questions for which the masculine world of the academy around me seemed to have expert and fluent answers. But I needed to think for myself—about pacifism and dissent and violence, about poetry and society, and about my own relationship to all these things. For about ten years I was reading in fierce snatches, scribbling in notebooks, writing poetry in fragments; I was looking desperately for clues, because if there were no clues then I thought I might be insane. I wrote in a notebook about this time:

> **Paralyzed by the sense that there exists a mesh of relationships—e.g., between my anger at the children, my sensual life, pacifism, sex (I mean sex in its broadest significance, not merely sexual desire)—an interconnectedness which, if I could see it, make it valid, would give me back myself, make it possible to function lucidly and passionately. Yet I grope in and out among these dark webs.**

I think I began at this point to feel that politics was not something "out there" but something "in here" and of the essence of my condition.

In the late fifties I was able to write, for the first time, directly about experiencing myself as a woman. The poem was jotted in fragments during children's naps, brief hours in a library, or at 3:00 A.M. after rising with a wakeful child. I despaired of doing any continuous work at this time. Yet I began to feel that my fragments and scraps had a common consciousness and a common theme, one that I would have been very unwilling to put on paper at an earlier time because I had been taught that poetry should be "universal," which meant, of course, nonfemale. Until then I had tried very much *not* to identify myself as a female poet. Over two years I wrote a ten-part poem called "Snapshots of a Daughter-in-Law" (1958–1960), in a longer looser mode than I'd ever trusted myself with before. It was an extraordinary relief to write that poem. It strikes me now as too literary, too dependent on allusion; I hadn't found the courage yet to do without authorities, or even to use the pronoun "I"—the woman in the poem is always "she." One section of it, No. 2, concerns a woman who thinks she is going mad; she is haunted by voices telling her to resist and rebel, voices that she can hear but not obey.

> **Banging the coffee-pot into the sink**
> **she hears the angels chiding, and looks out**
> **past the raked gardens to the sloppy sky.**
> **Only a week since They said: *Have no patience.***
>
> **The next time it was: *Be insatiable.***
> **Then: *Save yourself; others you cannot save.***
> **Sometimes she's let the tapstream scald her arm,**
> **a match burn to her thumbnail,**
>
> **or held her hand above the kettle's snout**
> **right in the woolly steam. They are probably angels,**
> **since nothing hurts her anymore, except**
> **each morning's grit blowing into her eyes.**

The poem "Orion," written five years later, is a poem of reconnection with a part of myself I had felt I was losing—the active principle, the energetic imagination, the "half-brother" whom I projected, as I had for many years, into the constellation Orion. It's no accident that the words "cold and egotistical" appear in this poem, and are applied to myself.

Far back when I went zig-zagging
through tamarack pastures
you were my genius, you
my cast-iron Viking, my helmed
lion-heart king in prison.
Years later now you're young

my fierce half-brother, staring
down from that simplified west
your breast open, your belt dragged down
by an oldfashioned thing, a sword
the last bravado you won't give over
though it weighs you down as you stride

and the stars in it are dim
and maybe have stopped burning.
But you burn, and I know it;
as I throw back my head to take you in
an old transfusion happens again:
divine astronomy is nothing to it.

Indoors I bruise and blunder,
break faith, leave ill enough
alone, a dead child born in the dark.
Night cracks up over the chimney,
pieces of time, frozen geodes
come showering down in the grate.

A man reaches behind my eyes
and finds them empty
a woman's head turns away
from my head in the mirror
children are dying my death
and eating crumbs of my life.

Pity is not your forte.
Calmly you ache up there

pinned aloft in your crow's nest,
my speechless pirate!
You take it all for granted
and when I look you back

it's with a starlike eye
shooting its cold and egotistical spear
where it can do least damage.
Breathe deep! No hurt, no pardon
out here in the cold with you
you with your back to the wall.

The choice still seemed to be between "love"—womanly, maternal love, altruistic love—a love defined and ruled by the weight of an entire culture; and egotism—a force directed by men into creation, achievement, ambition, often at the expense of others, but justifiably so. For weren't they men, and wasn't that their destiny as womanly, selfless love was ours? We know now that the alternatives are false ones—that the word "love" is itself in need of re-vision.

There is a companion poem to "Orion," written three years later, in which at last the woman in the poem and the woman writing the poem become the same person. It is called "Planetarium," and it was written after a visit to a real planetarium, where I read an account of the work of Caroline Herschel, the astronomer, who worked with her brother William, but whose name remained obscure, as his did not.

Thinking of Caroline Herschel, 1750–1848, astronomer, sister of William; and others

A woman in the shape of a monster
a monster in the shape of a woman
the skies are full of them

a woman   "in the snow
among the Clocks and instruments
or measuring the ground with poles"

in her 98 years to discover
8 comets

she whom the moon ruled
like us
levitating into the night sky
riding the polished lenses

Galaxies of women, there
doing penance for impetuousness
ribs chilled

in those spaces   of the mind

An eye,
  "virile, precise and absolutely certain"
  from the mad webs of Uranusborg
                    encountering the NOVA

every impulse of light exploding
from the core
as life flies out of us

      Tycho whispering at last
      "Let me not seem to have lived in vain"

What we see, we see
and seeing is changing

the light that shrivels a mountain
and leaves a man alive

Heartbeat of the pulsar
heart sweating through my body

The radio impulse
pouring in from Taurus

   I am bombarded yet   I stand

I have been standing all my life in the
direct path of a battery of signals
the most accurately transmitted most
untranslatable language in the universe
I am a galactic cloud so deep   so invo-
luted that a light wave could take 15
years to travel through me   And has
taken   I am an instrument in the shape
of a woman trying to translate pulsations
into images   for the relief of the body
and the reconstruction of the mind.

In closing I want to tell you about a dream I had last summer. I dreamed I was asked to read my poetry at a mass
women's meeting, but when I began to read, what came out
were the lyrics of a blues song. I share this dream with you
because it seemed to me to say something about the problems
and the future of the woman writer, and probably of women
in general. The awakening of consciousness is not like the
crossing of a frontier—one step and you are in another country. Much of women's poetry has been of the nature of the
blues song: a cry of pain, of victimization, or a lyric of se-
duction. And today, much poetry by women—and prose for
that matter—is charged with anger. I think we need to go
through that anger, and we will betray our own reality if we
try, as Virginia Woolf was trying, for an objectivity, a detach-

ment, that would make us sound more like Jane Austen or Shakespeare. We know more than Jane Austen or Shakespeare knew: more than Jane Austen because our lives are more complex, more than Shakespeare because we know more about the lives of women—Jane Austen and Virginia Woolf included.

Both the victimization and the anger experienced by women are real, and have real sources, everywhere in the environment, built into society, language, the structures of thought. They will go on being tapped and explored by poets, among others. We can neither deny them, nor will we rest there. A new generation of women poets is already working out of the psychic energy released when women begin to move out towards what the feminist philosopher Mary Daly has described as the "new space" on the "boundaries of patriarchy." Women are speaking to and of women in these poems, out of a newly released courage to name, to love each other, to share risk and grief and celebration.

To the eye of a feminist, the work of Western male poets writing in the 1970s reveals a deep, fatalistic pessimism as to the possibilities of change, whether societal or personal, along with a familiar and threadbare use of women (and nature) as redemptive on the one hand, threatening on the other; and a new tide of phallocentric sadism and overt woman-hating that matches the sexual brutality of recent films. "Political" poetry by men remains stranded amid the struggles for power among male groups; in condemning U.S. imperialism or the Chilean junta the poet can claim to speak for the oppressed while remaining, as male, part of a system of sexual oppression. The enemy is always outside the self, the struggle somewhere else. The mood of isolation, self-pity, and self-imitation that pervades "nonpolitical" poetry suggests that a profound change in masculine consciousness will have to precede any new male poetic—or other—inspiration. The creative energy of patriarchy is fast running out; what remains is its self-generating energy for destruction. As women, we have our work cut out for us.

1971

Women and Honor:
Some Notes on Lying

"*I wrote these notes in an effort to make myself more honest, and to decipher the terrible negative power of the lie in relationships between women*" (AR, 1979). *They were first read at the Women Writers' Workshop, founded and directed by Beverley Tanenhaus, at Hartwick College, Oneonta, New York, in June 1975. They were published as a pamphlet by Motheroot Press in Pittsburgh (1977); in* Heresies: A Feminist Magazine of Art and Politics *1, no. 1 (January 1977); in a French translation by the Québecois feminist press Les Éditions du Remue-Ménage (1979); and by Onlywomen Press in London.*

(These notes are concerned with relationships between and among women. When "personal relationship" is referred to, I mean a relationship between two women. It will be clear in what follows when I am talking about women's relationships with men.)

The old, male idea of honor. A man's "word" sufficed—to other men—without guarantee.

"Our Land Free, Our Men Honest, Our Women Fruitful"—
a popular colonial toast in America.

Male honor also having something to do with killing: *I could
not love thee, Dear, so much / Lov'd I not Honour more* ("To Lu-
casta, On Going to the Wars"). Male honor as something
needing to be avenged: hence, the duel.

Women's honor, something altogether else: virginity,
chastity, fidelity to a husband. Honesty in women has not been
considered important. We have been depicted as generically
whimsical, deceitful, subtle, vacillating. And we have been rewarded for lying.

Men have been expected to tell the truth about facts, not
about feelings. They have not been expected to talk about feelings at all.

Yet even about facts they have continually lied.

We assume that politicians are without honor. We read their
statements trying to crack the code. The scandals of their politics: not that men in high places lie, only that they do so with
such indifference, so endlessly, still expecting to be believed.
We are accustomed to the contempt inherent in the political lie.

———————

To discover that one has been lied to in a personal relationship, however, leads one to feel a little crazy.

———————

Lying is done with words, and also with silence.

The woman who tells lies in her personal relationships may
or may not plan or invent her lying. She may not even think of
what she is doing in a calculated way.

A subject is raised that the liar wishes buried. She has to go
downstairs, her parking meter will have run out. Or, there is
a telephone call she ought to have made an hour ago.

She is asked, point-blank, a question which may lead into painful talk: "How do you feel about what is happening between us?" Instead of trying to describe her feelings in their ambiguity and confusion, she asks, "How do *you* feel?" The other, because she is trying to establish a ground of openness and trust, begins describing her own feelings. Thus the liar learns more than she tells.

And she may also tell herself a lie: that she is concerned with the other's feelings, not with her own.

But the liar is concerned with her own feelings.

The liar lives in fear of losing control. She cannot even desire a relationship without manipulation, since to be vulnerable to another person means for her the loss of control.

The liar has many friends, and leads an existence of great loneliness.

The liar often suffers from amnesia. Amnesia is the silence of the unconscious.

To lie habitually, as a way of life, is to lose contact with the unconscious. It is like taking sleeping pills, which confer sleep but blot out dreaming. The unconscious wants truth. It ceases to speak to those who want something else more than truth.

In speaking of lies, we come inevitably to the subject of truth. There is nothing simple or easy about this idea. There is no "the truth," "a truth"—truth is not one thing, or even a system. It is an increasing complexity. The pattern of the carpet is a surface. When we look closely, or when we become weavers, we learn of the tiny multiple threads unseen in the overall pattern, the knots on the underside of the carpet.

This is why the effort to speak honestly is so important. Lies are usually attempts to make everything simpler—for the liar—than it really is, or ought to be.

In lying to others we end up lying to ourselves. We deny the importance of an event, or a person, and thus deprive ourselves of a part of our lives. Or we use one piece of the past or present to screen out another. Thus we lose faith even with our own lives.

The unconscious wants truth, as the body does. The complexity and fecundity of dreams come from the complexity and fecundity of the unconscious struggling to fulfill that desire. The complexity and fecundity of poetry come from the same struggle.

An honorable human relationship—that is, one in which two people have the right to use the word "love"—is a process, delicate, violent, often terrifying to both persons involved, a process of refining the truths they can tell each other.

It is important to do this because it breaks down human self-delusion and isolation.

It is important to do this because in so doing we do justice to our own complexity.

It is important to do this because we can count on so few people to go that hard way with us.

I come back to the questions of women's honor. Truthfulness has not been considered important for women, as long as we have remained physically faithful to a man, or chaste.

We have been expected to lie with our bodies: to bleach, redden, unkink or curl our hair, pluck eyebrows, shave armpits, wear padding in various places or lace ourselves, take little steps, glaze finger and toe nails, wear clothes that emphasized our helplessness.

We have been required to tell different lies at different

times, depending on what the men of the time needed to hear. The Victorian wife or the white southern lady, who were expected to have no sensuality, to "lie still"; the twentieth-century "free" woman who is expected to fake orgasms.

We have had the truth of our bodies withheld from us or distorted; we have been kept in ignorance of our most intimate places. Our instincts have been punished: clitoridectomies for "lustful" nuns or for "difficult" wives. It has been difficult, too, to know the lies of our complicity from the lies we believed.

The lie of the "happy marriage," of domesticity—we have been complicit, have acted out the fiction of a well-lived life, until the day we testify in court of rapes, beatings, psychic cruelties, public and private humiliations.

Patriarchal lying has manipulated women both through falsehood and through silence. Facts we needed have been withheld from us. False witness has been borne against us.

And so we must take seriously the question of truthfulness between women, truthfulness among women. As we cease to lie with our bodies, as we cease to take on faith what men have said about us, is a truly womanly idea of honor in the making?

———————————

Women have been forced to lie, for survival, to men. How to unlearn this among other women?

"Women have always lied to each other."
"Women have always whispered the truth to each other."
Both of these axioms are true.

"Women have always been divided against each other."
"Women have always been in secret collusion."
Both of these axioms are true.

In the struggle for survival we tell lies. To bosses, to prison guards, the police, men who have power over us, who legally own us and our children, lovers who need us as proof of their manhood.

There is a danger run by all powerless people: that we forget we are lying, or that lying becomes a weapon we carry over into relationships with people who do not have power over us.

I want to reiterate that when we talk about women and honor, or women and lying, we speak within the context of male lying, the lies of the powerful, the lie as false source of power.

Women have to think whether we want, in our relationships with each other, the kind of power that can be obtained through lying.

Women have been driven mad, "gaslighted," for centuries by the refutation of our experience and our instincts in a culture that validates only male experience. The truth of our bodies and our minds has been mystified to us. We therefore have a primary obligation to each other: not to undermine each others' sense of reality for the sake of expediency; not to gaslight each other.

Women have often felt insane when cleaving to the truth of our experience. Our future depends on the sanity of each of us, and we have a profound stake, beyond the personal, in the project of describing our reality as candidly and fully as we can to each other.

There are phrases that help us not to admit we are lying: "my privacy," "nobody's business but my own." The choices that underlie these phrases may indeed be justified; but we ought to think about the full meaning and consequences of such language.

Women's love for women has been represented almost entirely through silence and lies. The institution of heterosexuality has forced the lesbian to dissemble, or be labeled a pervert, a criminal, a sick or dangerous woman, etc., etc. The lesbian, then, has often been forced to lie, like the prostitute or the married women.

Does a life "in the closet"—lying, perhaps of necessity, about ourselves to bosses, landlords, clients, colleagues, family, because the law and public opinion are founded on a lie— does this, can it, spread into private life, so that lying (described as *discretion*) becomes an easy way to avoid conflict or complication? can it become a strategy so ingrained that it is used even with close friends and lovers?

Heterosexuality as an institution has also drowned in silence the erotic feelings between women. I myself lived half a lifetime in the lie of that denial. That silence makes us all, to some degree, into liars.

When a woman tells the truth she is creating the possibility for more truth around her.

The liar leads an existence of unutterable loneliness.

The liar is afraid.

But we are all afraid: without fear we become manic, hubristic, self-destructive. What is this particular fear that possesses the liar?

She is afraid that her own truths are not good enough.

She is afraid, not so much of prison guards or bosses, but of something unnamed within her.

The liar fears the void.

The void is not something created by patriarchy, or racism,

or capitalism. It will not fade away with any of them. It is part of every woman.

"The dark core," Virginia Woolf named it, writing of her mother. The dark core. It is beyond personality; beyond who loves us or hates us.

We begin out of the void, out of darkness and emptiness. It is part of the cycle understood by the old pagan religions, that materialism denies. Out of death, rebirth; out of nothing, something.

The void is the creatrix, the matrix. It is not mere hollowness and anarchy. But in women it has been identified with lovelessness, barrenness, sterility. We have been urged to fill our "emptiness" with children. We are not supposed to go down into the darkness of the core.

Yet, if we can risk it, the something born of that nothing is the beginning of our truth.

The liar in her terror wants to fill up the void, with anything. Her lies are a denial of her fear; a way of maintaining control.

―――――――――

Why do we feel slightly crazy when we realize we have been lied to in a relationship?

We take so much of the universe on trust. You tell me: "In 1950 I lived on the north side of Beacon Street in Somerville." You tell me: "She and I were lovers, but for months now we have only been good friends." You tell me: "It is seventy degrees outside and the sun is shining." Because I love you, because there is not even a question of lying between us, I take these accounts of the universe on trust: your address twenty-five years ago, your relationship with someone I know only by sight, this morning's weather. I fling unconscious tendrils of belief, like slender green threads, across statements such as these, statements made so unequivocally, which have no tone or shadow of tentativeness. I build them into the mosaic of my world. I allow my universe to change in minute, significant ways, on the basis of things you have said to me, of my trust in you.

I also have faith that you are telling me things it is important I should know; that you do not conceal facts from me in an effort to spare me, or yourself, pain.

Or, at the very least, that you will say, "There are things I am not telling you."

When we discover that someone we trusted can be trusted no longer, it forces us to reexamine the universe, to question the whole instinct and concept of trust. For a while, we are thrust back onto some bleak, jutting ledge, in a dark pierced by sheets of fire, swept by sheets of rain, in a world before kinship, or naming, or tenderness exist; we are brought close to formlessness.

———————————

The liar may resist confrontation, denying that she lied. Or she may use other language: forgetfulness, privacy, the protection of someone else. Or, she may bravely declare herself a coward. This allows her to go on lying, since that is what cowards do. She does not say, *I was afraid,* since this would open the question of other ways of handling her fear. It would open the question of what is actually feared.

She may say, *I didn't want to cause pain.* What she really did not want is to have to deal with the other's pain. The lie is a short-cut through another's personality.

———————————

Truthfulness, honor, is not something that springs ablaze of itself; it has to be created between people.

This is true in political situations. The quality and depth of the politics evolving from a group depends in very large part on their understanding of honor.

Much of what is narrowly termed "politics" seems to rest on a longing for certainty even at the cost of honesty, for an analysis that, once given, need not be reexamined. Such is the dead-endedness—for women—of Marxism in our time.

Truthfulness anywhere means a heightened complexity. But it is a movement into evolution. Women are only beginning to uncover our own truths; many of us would be grateful for some rest in that struggle, would be glad just to lie down with the sherds we have painfully unearthed, and be satisfied with those. Often I feel this like an exhaustion in my own body.

The politics worth having, the relationships worth having, demand that we delve still deeper.

––––––––––––

The possibilities that exist between two people, or among a group of people, are a kind of alchemy. They are the most interesting thing in life. The liar is someone who keeps losing sight of these possibilities.

When relationships are determined by manipulation, by the need for control, they may possess a dreary, bickering kind of drama, but they cease to be interesting. They are repetitious; the shock of human possibilities has ceased to reverberate through them.

When someone tells me a piece of the truth that has been withheld from me, and that I needed in order to see my life more clearly, it may bring acute pain, but it can also flood me with a cold, sea-sharp wash of relief. Often such truths come by accident, or from strangers.

It isn't that to have an honorable relationship with you, I have to understand everything, or tell you everything at once, or that I can know, beforehand, everything I need to tell you.

It means that most of the time I am eager, longing for the possibility of telling you. That these possibilities may seem frightening, but not destructive, to me. That I feel strong enough to hear your tentative and groping words. That we both know we are trying, all the time, to extend the possibilities of truth between us.

The possibility of life between us.

1975

Blood, Bread, and Poetry: The Location of the Poet

This talk was given for the Institute for the Humanities, University of Massachusetts, Amherst, as part of their 1983 series "Writers and Social Responsibility," and was originally published in the Massachusetts Review.

The Miami airport, summer 1983: a North American woman says to me, "You'll love Nicaragua: everyone there is a poet." I've thought many times of that remark, both while there and since returning home. Coming from a culture that encourages poets to think of ourselves as alienated from the sensibility of the general population, that casually and devastatingly marginalizes us (so far, no slave labor or torture for a political poem—just dead air, the white noise of the media jamming the poet's words)—coming from this dominant culture that so confuses us, telling us poetry is neither economically profitable nor politically effective and that political dissidence is destructive to art, coming from this culture that tells me I am destined to be a luxury, a decorative garnish on the buffet table of the university curriculum, the ceremonial occasion, the national celebration—what am I to make, I thought, of that remark? *You'll love Nicaragua: everyone there is a poet.* (Do I love poets in general? I immediately asked myself, thinking of poets I neither love nor would wish to see in charge of my country.) Is being a poet a guarantee that I will love a Marxist-Leninist revolution? Can't I travel simply as an American radical, a lesbian feminist, a citizen who opposes her government's wars against its own people and its intervention in other people's lands? And what effectiveness has the testimony of a poet returning from a revolution where "everyone is a poet" to a country where the possible credibility of poetry is not even seriously discussed?

Clearly, this well-meant remark triggered strong and complex feelings in me. And it provided, in a sense, the text on which I began to build my talk here tonight.

I was born at the brink of the Great Depression; I reached sixteen the year of Nagasaki and Hiroshima. The daughter of a Jewish father and a Protestant mother, I learned about the Holocaust first from newsreels of the liberation of the death camps. I was a young white woman who had never known hunger or homelessness, growing up in the suburbs of a deeply segregated city in which neighborhoods were also dictated along religious lines: Christian and Jewish. I lived sixteen years of my life secure in the belief that though cities could be bombed and civilian populations killed, the earth stood in its old indestructible way. The process through which nuclear annihilation was to become a part of all human calculation had already begun, but we did not live with that knowledge during the first sixteen years of my life. And a recurrent theme in much poetry I read was the indestructibility of poetry, the poem as a vehicle for personal immortality.

I had grown up hearing and reading poems from a very young age, first as sounds, repeated, musical, rhythmically satisfying in themselves, and the power of concrete, sensuously compelling images:

All night long they hunted
  And nothing did they find
But a ship a-sailing,
  A-sailing with the wind.
One said it was a ship,
  The other he said, Nay,
The third said it was a house
  With the chimney blown away;
And all the night they hunted
  And nothing did they find
But the moon a-gliding
  A-gliding with the wind. . . .

Tyger! Tyger! burning bright
  In the forest of the night,
What immortal hand or eye
  Dare frame thy fearful symmetry?

But poetry soon became more than music and images; it was also revelation, information, a kind of teaching. I believed I could learn from it—an unusual idea for a United States citizen, even a child. I thought it could offer clues, intimations, keys to questions that already stalked me, questions I could not even frame yet: *What is possible in this life? What does "love" mean, this thing that is so important? What is this other thing called "freedom" or "liberty"—is it like love, a feeling? What have human beings lived and suffered in the past? How am I going to live my life?* The fact that poets contradicted themselves and each other didn't baffle or alarm me. I was avid for everything I could get; my child's mind did not shut down for the sake of consistency.

I was angry with my friend,
I told my wrath, my wrath did end.
I was angry with my foe,
I told it not, my wrath did grow.

As an angry child, often urged to "curb my temper," I used to ponder those words of William Blake, but they slid first into my memory through their repetitions of sound, their ominous rhythms.

Another poem that I loved first as music, later pondered for what it could tell me about women and men and marriage, was Edwin Arlington Robinson's "Eros Turannos":

> **She fears him, and will always ask**
> **What fated her to choose him;**
> **She meets in his engaging mask**
> **All reasons to refuse him;**
> **But what she meets and what she fears**
> **Are less than are the downward years,**
> **Drawn slowly to the foamless weirs**
> **Of age, were she to lose him. . . .**

And, of course, I thought that the poets in the anthologies were the only real poets, that their being in the anthologies was proof of this, though some were classified as "great" and others as "minor." I owed much to those anthologies: *Silver Pennies;* the constant outflow of volumes edited by Louis Untermeyer; *The Cambridge Book of Poetry for Children;* Palgrave's *Golden Treasury;* the *Oxford Book of English Verse.* But I had no idea that they reflected the taste of a particular time or of particular kinds of people. I still believed that poets were inspired by some transcendent authority and spoke from some extraordinary height. I thought that the capacity to hook syllables together in a way that heated the blood was the sign of a universal vision.

Because of the attitudes surrounding me, the aesthetic ideology with which I grew up, I came into my twenties believing in poetry, in all art, as the expression of a higher world view, what the critic Edward Said has termed "a quasi-religious wonder, instead of a human sign to be understood in secular and social terms." The poet achieved "universality" and authority through tapping his, or occasionally her, own dreams, longings, fears, desires, and, out of this, "speaking as a man to men," as Wordsworth had phrased it. But my personal world view at sixteen, as at twenty-six, was itself being created by political conditions. I was not a man; I was white in a white-supremacist society; I was being educated from the perspective of a particular class; my father was an "assimilated" Southern Jew, my mother a southern Protestant; there were particular historical currents on which my consciousness would come together, piece by piece. My personal world view was shaped in part by the poetry I had read, a poetry written almost entirely by white Anglo-Saxon men, a few women, Celts and Frenchmen notwithstanding. Thus, no poetry in the Spanish language or from Africa or China or the Middle East. My personal world view, which like so many young people I carried as a conviction of my own uniqueness, was not original with me, but was, rather, my untutored and half-conscious rendering of the facts of blood and bread, the social and political forces of my time and place.

I was in college during the late 1940s and early 1950s. The thirties, a decade of economic desperation, social unrest, war, and also of affirmed political art, was receding behind the fogs of the Cold War, the selling of the nuclear family with the mother at home as its core, heightened activity by the FBI and CIA, a retreat by many artists from so-called "protest" art, witch-hunting among artists and intellectuals as well as in the State Department, anti-Semitism, scapegoating of homosexual men and lesbians, and in the 1953 electrocution of Ethel and Julius Rosenberg.

Francis Otto Matthiessen, a socialist and a homosexual,

was teaching literature at Harvard when I came there. One semester he lectured on five poets: Blake, Keats, Byron, Yeats, and Stevens. That class perhaps affected my life as a poet more than anything else that happened to me in college. Matthiessen had a passion for language, and he read aloud, made us memorize poems and recite them to him as part of the course. He also actually alluded to events in the outside world, the hope that eastern Europe could survive as an independent socialist force between the United States and the Soviet Union; he spoke of the current European youth movements as if they should matter to us. Poetry, in his classroom, never remained in the realm of pure textual criticism. Remember that this was in 1947 or 1948, that it was a rare teacher of literature at Harvard who referred to a world beyond the text, even though the classrooms were full of World War II veterans studying on the G.I. Bill of Rights—men who might otherwise never have gone to college, let alone Harvard, at all. Matthiessen committed suicide in the spring of my sophomore year.

Because of Yeats, who by then had become my idea of the Great Poet, the one who more than others could hook syllables together in a way that heated my blood, I took a course in Irish history. It was taught by a Boston Irish professor of Celtic, one of Harvard's tokens, whose father, it was said, had been a Boston policeman. He read poetry aloud in Gaelic and in English, sang us political ballads, gave us what amounted to a mini-education on British racism and imperialism, though the words were never mentioned. He also slashed at Irish self-romanticizing. People laughed about the Irish history course, said it must be full of football players. In and out of the Harvard Yard, the racism of Yankee Brahmin toward Boston Irish was never questioned, laced as it was with equally unquestioned class arrogance. Today, Irish Boston both acts out and takes the weight of New England racism against Black and Hispanic people. It was, strangely enough, through poetry that I first began to try to make sense of these things.

"Strangely enough," I say, because the reading of poetry in an elite academic institution is supposed to lead you—in the 1980s as back there in the early 1950s—not toward a criticism of society, but toward a professional career in which the anatomy of poems is studied dispassionately. Prestige, job security, money, and inclusion in an exclusive fraternity are where the academic study of literature is supposed to lead. Maybe I was lucky because I had started reading poetry so young, and not in school, and because I had been writing poems almost as long as I had been reading them. I should add that I was easily entranced by pure sound and still am, no matter what it is saying; and any poet who mixes the poetry of the actual world with the poetry of sound interests and excites me more than I am able to say. In my student years, it was Yeats who seemed to do this better than anyone else. There were lines of Yeats that were to ring in my head for years:

> **Many times man lives and dies**
> **Between his two eternities,**
> **That of race and that of soul,**
> **And ancient Ireland knew it all. . . .**
>
> **Did she in touching that lone wing**
> **Recall the years before her mind**
> **Became a bitter, an abstract thing**
> **Her thought some popular enmity:**
> **Blind and leader of the blind**
> **Drinking the foul ditch where they lie?**

I could hazard the guess that all the most impassioned, seductive arguments against the artist's involvement in politics can be found in Yeats. It was this dialogue between art and politics that excited me in his work, along with the sound of his language—never his elaborate mythological systems. I know I learned two things from his poetry, and those two things were at war with each other. One was that poetry can root itself in politics. Even if it defends privilege, even if it deplores political rebellion and revolution, it can, may have to, account for itself politically, consciously situate itself amid political conditions, without sacrificing intensity of language. The other, that politics leads to "bitterness" and "abstractness" of mind, makes women shrill and hysterical, and is finally a waste of beauty and talent: "Too long a sacrifice / can make a stone of the heart." There was absolutely nothing in the literary canon I knew to counter the second idea. Elizabeth Barrett Browning's anti-slavery and feminist poetry, H.D.'s anti-war and woman-identified poetry, like the radical—yes, revolutionary—work of Langston Hughes and Muriel Rukeyser, were still buried by the academic literary canon. But the first idea was extremely important to me: a poet—one who was apparently certified—could actually write about political themes, could weave the names of political activists into a poem:

> **MacDonagh and MacBride**
> **And Connally and Pearce**
> **Now and in time to come**
> **Wherever green is worn**
> **Are changed, changed utterly:**
> **A terrible beauty is born.**

As we all do when young and searching for what we can't even name yet, I took what I could use where I could find it. When the ideas or forms we need are banished, we seek their residues wherever we can trace them. But there was one major problem with this. I had been born a woman, and I was trying to think and act as if poetry—and the possibility of making poems—were a universal—a gender-neutral—realm. In the universe of the masculine paradigm, I naturally absorbed ideas about women, sexuality, power from the subjectivity of male poets—Yeats not least among them. The dissonance between these images and the daily events of my own life demanded a constant footwork of imagination, a kind of perpetual translation, and an unconscious fragmentation of identity: woman from poet. Every group that lives under the naming and image-making power of a dominant culture is at risk from this mental fragmentation and needs an art that can resist it.

But at the middle of the fifties I had no very clear idea of my positioning in the world or even that such an idea was an important resource for a writer to have. I knew that marriage and motherhood, experiences that were supposed to be truly, naturally, womanly, often left me feeling unfit, disempowered, adrift. But I had never had to think about bread itself as a primary issue; and what I knew of blood was that I was white and that white was better off. Much as my parents had worried about questions of social belonging and acceptability, I had never had to swallow rage or humiliation to earn a paycheck. The literature I had read only rarely suggested that for many people it is a common, everyday fact of life to be hungry. I thought I was well educated. In that Cold War atmosphere, which has never really ended, we heard a lot about the "indoctrinating" of people in the Soviet Union, the egregious rewriting of history to conform to Communist dogma. But, like most Americans, I had been taught a particular version of our history, the version of the propertied white male; and in my early twenties I did not even realize this. As a younger and then an older woman, growing up in the white mainstream American culture, I was destined to piece together, for the rest of my life, laboriously and with much in my training against me, the history that really concerned me, on which I was to rely as a poet, the only history upon which, both as a woman and a poet, I could find any grounding at all: the history of the dispossessed.

It was in the pain and confusion of that inward wrenching of the self, which I experienced directly as a young woman in the fifties, that I started to feel my way backward to an earlier splitting: the covert and overt taboos against Black people, which had haunted my earliest childhood. And I began searching for some clue or key to life, not only in poetry but in political writers. The writers I found were Mary Wollstonecraft, Simone de Beauvoir, and James Baldwin. Each of them helped me to realize that what had seemed simply "the way things are" could actually be a social construct, advantageous to some people and detrimental to others, and that these constructs could be criticized and changed. The myths and obsessions of gender, the myths and obsessions of race, the violent exercise of power in these relationships could be identified, their territories could be mapped. They were not simply part of my private turmoil, a secret misery, an individual failure. I did not yet know what I, a white woman, might have to say about the racial obsessions of white consciousness. But I did begin to resist the apparent splitting of poet from woman, thinker from woman, and to write what I feared was political poetry. And in this I had very little encouragement from the literary people I knew, but I did find courage and vindication in words like Baldwin's: "Any real change implies the breakup of the world as one has always known it, the loss of all that gave one an identity, the end of safety." I don't know why I found these words encouraging—perhaps because they made me feel less alone.

Mary Wollstonecraft had seen eighteenth-century middle-class Englishwomen brain-starved and emotionally malnourished through denial of education; her plea was to treat women's minds as respectfully as men's—to admit women as equals into male culture. Simone de Beauvoir showed how the male perception of Woman as Other dominated European culture, keeping "woman" entrapped in myths that robbed her of her independent being and value. James Baldwin insisted that *all* culture was politically significant, and described the complexity of living with integrity as a Black person, an artist in a white-dominated culture, whether as an African-American growing up in Harlem, U.S.A., or as an African in a country emerging from a history of colonialism. He also alluded to "that as yet unwritten history of the Negro woman"; and he wrote in 1954 in an essay on Gide that "when men [heterosexual or homosexual] can no longer love women they also cease to love or respect or trust each other, which makes their isolation complete." And he was the first writer I read who suggested that racism was poisonous to white as well as destructive to Black people.

The idea of freedom—so much invoked during World War II—had become pretty abstract politically in the fifties. Freedom—then as now—was supposed to be what the Western democracies believed in and the "Iron Curtain" Soviet-bloc countries were deprived of. The existentialist philosophers who were beginning to be read and discussed among young American intellectuals spoke of freedom as something connected with revolt. But in reading de Beauvoir and Baldwin, I began to taste the concrete reality of being unfree, how continuous and permeating and corrosive a condition it is, and how it is maintained through culture as much as through the use of force.

I am telling you this from a backward perspective, from where I stand now. At the time I could not have summed up the effect these writers had on me. I only knew that I was reading them with the same passion and need that I brought to poetry, that they were beginning to penetrate my life; I was beginning to feel as never before that I had some foothold, some way of seeing, which helped me to ask the questions I needed to ask.

But there were many voices then, as there are now, warning the North American artist against "mixing politics with art." I have been trying to retrace, to delineate, these arguments, which carry no weight for me now because I recognize them as the political declarations of privilege. There is the falsely mystical view of art that assumes a kind of supernatural inspiration, a possession by universal forces unrelated to questions of power and privilege or the artist's relation to bread and blood. In this view, the channel of art can only become clogged and misdirected by the artist's concern with merely temporary and local disturbances. The song is higher than the struggle, and the artist must choose between politics—here defined as earthbound factionalism, corrupt power struggles—and art, which exists on some transcendent plane. This view of literature has dominated literary criticism in England and America for nearly a century. In the fifties and early sixties there was much shaking of heads if an artist was found "meddling in politics"; art was mystical and universal, but the artist was also, apparently, irresponsible and emotional and politically naïve.

In North America, moreover, "politics" is mostly a dirty word, associated with low-level wheeling and dealing, with manipulation. (There is nothing North Americans seem to fear so much as manipulation, probably because at some level we know that we belong to a deeply manipulative system.) "Politics" also suggested, certainly in the fifties, the Red Menace, Jewish plots, spies, malcontents conspiring to overthrow democracy, "outside agitators" stirring up perfectly contented

Black and/or working people. Such activities were dangerous and punishable, and in the McCarthy era there was a great deal of fear abroad. The writer Meridel LeSueur was blacklisted, hounded by the FBI, her books banned; she was dismissed from job after job—teaching, waitressing—because the FBI intimidated her students and employers. A daughter of Tillie Olsen recalls going with her mother in the 1950s to the Salvation Army to buy heavy winter clothes because the family had reason to believe that Leftists in the San Francisco Bay Area would be rounded up and taken to detention camps farther north. These are merely two examples of politically committed writers who did survive that particular repression—many never recovered from it.

Perhaps many white North Americans fear an overtly political art because it might persuade us emotionally of what we think we are "rationally" against; it might get to us on a level we have lost touch with, undermine the safety we have built for ourselves, remind us of what is better left forgotten. This fear attributes real power to the voices of passion and of poetry that connect us with all that is not simply white chauvinist/male supremacist/straight/puritanical—with what is "dark," "effeminate," "inverted," "primitive," "volatile," "sinister." Yet we are told that political poetry, for example, is doomed to grind down into mere rhetoric and jargon, to become one-dimensional, simplistic, vituperative; that in writing "protest literature"—that is, writing from a perspective that may not be male, or white, or heterosexual, or middle-class—we sacrifice the "universal"; that in writing of injustice we are limiting our scope, "grinding a political axe." So political poetry is suspected of immense subversive power, yet accused of being, by definition, bad writing, impotent, lacking in breadth. No wonder if the North American poet finds herself or himself slightly crazed by the double messages.

By 1956, I had begun dating each of my poems by year. I did this because I was finished with the idea of a poem as a single, encapsulated event, a work of art complete in itself; I knew my life was changing, my work was changing, and I needed to indicate to readers my sense of being engaged in a long, continuing process. It seems to me now that this was an oblique political statement—a rejection of the dominant critical idea that the poem's text should be read as separate from the poet's everyday life in the world. It was a declaration that placed poetry in a historical continuity, not above or outside history.

In my own case, as soon as I published—in 1963—a book of poems that was informed by any conscious sexual politics, I was told, in print, that this work was "bitter," "personal"; that I had sacrificed the sweetly flowing measures of my earlier books for a ragged line and a coarsened voice. It took me a long time not to hear those voices internally whenever I picked up my pen. But I was writing at the beginning of a decade of political revolt and hope and activism. Out of the Black Civil Rights movement, amid the marches and sit-ins in the streets and on campuses, a new generation of Black writers began to speak—and older generations to be reprinted and reread; poetry readings were infused with the spirit of collective rage and hope. As part of the movement against United States militarism and imperialism, white poets also were writing and reading aloud poems addressing the war in Southeast Asia. In many of these poems you sensed the poet's desperation in trying to encompass in words the reality of napalm, the "pacification" of villages, trying to make vivid in poetry what seemed to have minimal effect when shown on television. But there was little location of the self, the poet's own identity as a man or woman. As I wrote in another connection, "The enemy is always outside the self, the struggle somewhere else."

I had—perhaps through reading de Beauvoir and Baldwin—some nascent idea that "Vietnam and the lovers' bed," as I phrased it then, were connected; I found myself, in the late sixties, trying to describe those relations in poetry. Even before I called myself a feminist or a lesbian, I felt driven—for my own sanity—to bring together in my poems the political world "out there"—the world of children dynamited or napalmed, of the urban ghetto and militarist violence, and the supposedly private, lyrical world of sex and of male/female relationships.

I began teaching at the City College of New York in a program intended to compensate ghetto students for the inadequacy of the city's public schools. Among staff and students, and in the larger academic community, there were continual debates over the worth and even the linguistic existence of Black English, the expressive limits and social uses of Standard English—the politics of language. As a poet, I had learned much about both the value and the constraints of convention: the reassurances of traditional structures and the necessity to break from them in recognition of new experience. I felt more and more urgently the dynamic between poetry as language and poetry as a kind of action, probing, burning, stripping, placing itself in dialogue with others out beyond the individual self.

By the end of the 1960s an autonomous movement of women was declaring that "the personal is political." That statement was necessary because in other political movements of that decade the power relation of men to women, the question of women's roles and men's roles, had been dismissed—often contemptuously—as the sphere of personal life. Sex itself was not seen as political, except for interracial sex. Women were now talking about domination, not just in terms of economic exploitation, militarism, colonialism, imperialism, but within the family, in marriage, in child rearing, in the heterosexual act itself. Breaking the mental barrier that separated private from public life felt in itself like an enormous surge toward liberation. For women thus engaged, every aspect of life was on the line. We began naming and acting on issues we had been told were trivial, unworthy of mention: rape by husbands or lovers; the boss's hand groping the employee's breast; the woman beaten in her home with no place to go; the woman sterilized when she sought an abortion; the lesbian penalized for her private life by loss of her child, her lease, her job. We pointed out that women's unpaid work in the home is central to every economy, capitalist or socialist. And in the crossover between personal and political, we were also pushing at the limits of experience reflected in literature, certainly in poetry.

To write directly and overtly as a woman, out of a woman's body and experience, to take women's existence seriously as theme and source for art, was something I had been hungering to do, needing to do, all my writing life. It placed me nakedly face to face with both terror and anger; it did indeed *imply the breakdown of the world as I had always known it, the end of safety,* to paraphrase Baldwin again. But it released tremendous energy in me, as in many other women, to have that way of writing affirmed and validated in a growing political community. I felt for the first time the closing of the gap between poet and woman.

Women have understood that we needed an art of our own: to remind us of our history and what we might be; to show us our true faces—all of them, including the unacceptable; to speak of what has been muffled in code or silence; to make concrete the values our movement was bringing forth out of consciousness raising, speakouts, and activism. But we were—and are—living and writing not only within a women's community. We are trying to build a political and cultural movement in the heart of capitalism, in a country where racism assumes every form of physical, institutional, and psychic violence, and in which more than one person in seven lives below the poverty line. The United States feminist movement is rooted in the United States, a nation with a particular history of hostility both to art and to socialism, where art has been encapsulated as a commodity, a salable artifact, something to be taught in MFA programs, that requires a special staff of "arts administrators"; something you "gotta have" without exactly knowing why. As a lesbian, feminist, poet, and writer, I need to understand how this *location* affects me, along with the realities of blood and bread within this nation.

"As a woman I have no country. As a woman I want no country. As a woman my country is the whole world." These words, written by Virginia Woolf in her feminist and anti-fascist book *Three Guineas*, we dare not take out of context to justify a false transcendence, an irresponsibility toward the cultures and geopolitical regions in which we are rooted. Woolf was attacking—as a feminist—patriotism, nationalism, the values of the British patriarchal establishment for which so many wars have been fought all over the world. Her feminism led her by the end of her life to anti-imperialism. As women, I think it essential that we admit and explore our cultural identities, our national identities, even as we reject the patriotism, jingoism, nationalism offered to us as "the American way of life." Perhaps the most arrogant and malevolent delusion of North American power—of white Western power—has been the delusion of destiny, that white is at the center, that white is endowed with some right or mission to judge and ransack and assimilate and destroy the values of other peoples. As a white feminist artist in the United States, I do not want to perpetuate that chauvinism, but I still have to struggle with its pervasiveness in culture, its residues in myself.

Working as I do in the context of a movement in which artists are encouraged to address political and ethical questions, I have felt released to a large degree from the old separation of art from politics. But the presence of that separation "out there" in North American life is one of many impoverishing forces of capitalist patriarchy. I began to sense what it might be to live, and to write poetry, as a woman, in a society that took seriously the necessity for poetry, when I read Margaret Randall's anthology of contemporary Cuban women poets *Breaking the Silences*. This book had a powerful effect on me—the consistently high level of poetry, the diversity of voices, the sense of the poets' connections with world and community, and, in their individual statements, the affirmation of an organic relation between poetry and social transformation:

> **Things move so much around you.**
> **Even your country has changed. You yourself have**
> **changed it.**
>
> **And the soul, will it change? You must change it.**
> **Who will tell you otherwise?**
> **Will it be a desolate journey?**
> **Will it be tangible, languid**
> **without a hint of violence?**
> **As long as you are the person you are today**
> **being yesterday's person as well,**
> **you will be tomorrow's . . .**
> **the one who lives and dies**
> **to live like this.**

It was partly because of that book that I went to Nicaragua. I seized the opportunity when it arose, not because I thought that everyone would be a poet, but because I had been feeling more and more ill informed, betrayed by the coverage of Central America in the United States media. I wanted to know what the Sandinistas believed they stood for, what directions they wanted to take in their very young, imperiled revolution. But I also wanted to get a sense of what art might mean in a society committed to values other than profit and consumerism. What was constantly and tellingly manifested was a *belief* in art, not as commodity, not as luxury, not as suspect activity, but as a precious resource to be made available to all, one necessity for the rebuilding of a scarred, impoverished, and still-bleeding country. And returning home I had to ask myself: What happens to the heart of the artist, here in North America? What toll is taken of art when it is separated from the social fabric? How is art curbed, how are we made to feel useless and helpless, in a system that so depends on our alienation?

Alienation—not just from the world of material conditions, of power to make things happen or stop happening. Alienation from our own roots, whatever they are, the memories, dreams, stories, the language, history, the sacred materials of art. In *A Gathering of Spirit,* an anthology of writing and art by North American Indian women, a poem by the Chicana/American Indian poet Anita Valerio reasserts the claim to a complex historical and cultural identity, the selves who are both of the past and of tomorrow:

There is the cab driver root and elevator
root, there is the water
root of lies   The root of speech hidden in the secretary's
marinated tongue   There is the ocean
root and seeing
root, heart and belly root, antelope
roots hidden in hills   There is the root
of the billy club/beginning with electric drums . . .
    root of hunters   smoky

ascensions into heaven   trails
  beat out of ice   There is the root
of homecoming   The house my grandfather built first   I see
him   standing in his black
hat beating the snake with a stick
  There is the root shaped
by spirits speaking
in the lodge   There is the root you don't
want to hear and the one that hides
from you under the couch. . . .

  Root of teeth and
the nape of the goat   oranges,   fog
written on a camera   There is the carrot owl hunting
for her hat in the wind   moccasins
         of the blue deer
 flashing
in the doorknob. . . .
  There is the root of sex eating
pound cake in the kitchen   crumbs
       crumbs
        alibis
crumbs
a convict astroprojects   She is
picking up her torches, picking up her psalms, her
necklaces

I write in full knowledge that the majority of the world's il-
literates are women, that I live in a technologically advanced
country where 40 percent of the people can barely read and 20
percent are functionally illiterate. I believe that these facts
are directly connected to the fragmentations I suffer in myself,
that we are all in this together. Because I can write at all—and
I think of all the ways women especially have been prevented
from writing—because my words are read and taken seriously,

because I see my work as part of something larger than my own life or the history of literature, I feel a responsibility to keep searching for teachers who can help me widen and deepen the sources and examine the ego that speaks in my poems—not for political "correctness," but for ignorance, solipsism, laziness, dishonesty, automatic writing. I look everywhere for signs of that fusion I have glimpsed in the women's movement, and most recently in Nicaragua. I turn to Toni Cade Bambara's *The Salt Eaters* or Ama Ata Aidoo's *Our Sister Killjoy* or James Baldwin's *Just above My Head*; to paintings by Frida Kahlo or Jacob Lawrence; to poems by Dionne Brand or Judy Grahn or Audre Lorde or Nancy Morejón; to the music of Nina Simone or Mary Watkins. This kind of art—like the art of so many others uncanonized in the dominant culture— is not produced as a commodity, but as part of a long conversation with the elders and with the future. (And, yes, I do live and work believing in a future.) Such artists draw on a tradition in which political struggle and spiritual continuity are meshed. Nothing need be lost, no beauty sacrificed. The heart does not turn to a stone.

1983

Notes toward a Politics
of Location

*I was invited to give this talk in Utrecht, Holland, June 1984,
at the First Summer School of Critical Semiotics, Conference
on Women, Feminist Identity and Society in the 1980s. The
paper was first published in* Women, Feminist Identity and
Society in the 1980s: Selected Papers, *edited by Myriam Díaz-
Diocaretz and Iris Zavala (Amsterdam/Philadelphia: John
Benjamins, 1985).*

I am to speak these words in Europe, but I have been searching for them in the United States of America. A few years ago
I would have spoken of the common oppression of women, the
gathering movement of women around the globe, the hidden
history of women's resistance and bonding, the failure of all
previous politics to recognize the universal shadow of patriarchy, the belief that women now, in a time of rising consciousness and global emergency, may join across all national
and cultural boundaries to create a society free of domination, in which "sexuality, politics, . . . work, . . . intimacy . . .
thinking itself will be transformed."

I would have spoken these words as a feminist who "happened" to be a white United States citizen, conscious of my

government's proven capacity for violence and arrogance of power, but as self-separated from that government, quoting without second thought Virginia Woolf's statement in *Three Guineas* that "as a woman my country is the whole world."

This is not what I come here to say in 1984. I come here with notes but without absolute conclusions. This is not a sign of loss of faith or hope. These notes are the marks of a struggle to keep moving, a struggle for accountability.

———————

Beginning to write, then getting up. Stopped by the movements of a huge early bumblebee that has somehow gotten inside this house and is reeling, bumping, stunning itself against windowpanes and sills. I open the front door and speak to it, trying to attract it outside. It is looking for what it needs, just as I am, and, like me, it has gotten trapped in a place where it cannot fulfill its own life. I could open the jar of honey on the kitchen counter, and perhaps it would take honey from that jar; but its life process, its work, its mode of being cannot be fulfilled inside this house.

And I, too, have been bumping my way against glassy panes, falling half-stunned, gathering myself up and crawling, then again taking off, searching.

I don't hear the bumblebee any more, and I leave the front door. I sit down and pick up a secondhand, faintly annotated student copy of Marx's *The German Ideology,* which "happens" to be lying on the table.

———————

I will speak these words in Europe, but I am having to search for them in the United States of North America. When I was ten or eleven, early in World War II, a girlfriend and I used to write each other letters that we addressed like this:

Adrienne Rich
14 Edgevale Road
Baltimore, Maryland
The United States of America
The Continent of North America
The Western Hemisphere
The Earth
The Solar System
The Universe

You could see your own house as a tiny fleck on an ever-widening landscape, or as the center of it all from which the circles expanded into the infinite unknown.

It is that question of feeling at the center that gnaws at me now. At the center of what?

As a woman I have a country; as a woman I cannot divest myself of that country merely by condemning its government or by saying three times "As a woman my country is the whole world." Tribal loyalties aside, and even if nation-states are now just pretexts used by multinational conglomerates to serve their interests, I need to understand how a place on the map is also a place in history within which as a woman, a Jew, a lesbian, a feminist I am created and trying to create.

Begin, though, not with a continent or a country or a house, but with the geography closest in—the body. Here at least I know I exist, that living human individual whom the young Marx called "the first premise of all human history." But it was not as a Marxist that I turned to this place, back from philosophy and literature and science and theology in which I had looked for myself in vain. It was as a radical feminist.

The politics of pregnability and motherhood. The politics of orgasm. The politics of rape and incest, of abortion, birth control, forcible sterilization. Of prostitution and marital sex. Of what had been named sexual liberation. Of prescriptive heterosexuality. Of lesbian existence.

And Marxist feminists were often pioneers in this work. But for many women I knew, the need to begin with the female body—our own—was understood not as applying a Marxist principle *to* women, but as locating the grounds from which to speak with authority *as* women. Not to transcend this body, but to reclaim it. To reconnect our thinking and speaking with the body of this particular living human individual, a woman. Begin, we said, with the material, with matter, mma, madre, mutter, moeder, modder, etc., etc.

—————

Begin with the material. Pick up again the long struggle against lofty and privileged abstraction. Perhaps this is the core of revolutionary process, whether it calls itself Marxist or Third World or feminist or all three. Long before the nineteenth century, the empirical witch of the European Middle Ages, trusting her senses, practicing her tried remedies against the anti-material, anti-sensuous, anti-empirical dogmas of the Church. Dying for that, by the millions. "A female-led peasant rebellion"?—in any event, a rebellion against the idolatry of pure ideas, the belief that ideas have a life of their own and float along above the heads of ordinary people—women, the poor, the uninitiated.

Abstractions severed from the doings of living people, fed back to people as slogans.

Theory—the seeing of patterns, showing the forest as well as the trees—theory can be a dew that rises from the earth and collects in the rain cloud and returns to earth over and over. But if it doesn't smell of the earth, it isn't good for the earth.

I wrote a sentence just now and x'd it out. In it I said that women have always understood the struggle against free-floating abstraction even when they were intimidated by abstract ideas. I don't want to write that kind of sentence now, the sentence that begins "Women have always. . . ." We started by rejecting the sentences that began "Women have always had an instinct for mothering" or "Women have always and everywhere been in subjugation to men." If we have learned anything in these years of late twentieth-century feminism, it's that that "always" blots out what we really need to know: When, where, and under what conditions has the statement been true?

The absolute necessity to raise these questions in the world: where, when, and under what conditions have women acted and been acted on, as women? Wherever people are struggling against subjection, the specific subjection of women, through our location in a female body, from now on has to be addressed. The necessity to go on speaking of it, refusing to let the discussion go on as before, speaking where silence has been advised and enforced, not just about our subjection, but about our active presence and practice as women. We believed (I go on believing) that the liberation of women is a wedge driven into all other radical thought, can open out the structures of resistance, unbind the imagination, connect what's been dangerously disconnected. Let us pay attention now, we said, to women: let men and women make a conscious act of attention when women speak; let us insist on kinds of process that allow more women to speak; let us get back to earth—not as paradigm for "women," but as place of location.

Perhaps we need a moratorium on saying "the body." For it's also possible to abstract "the" body. When I write "the body," I see nothing in particular. To write "my body" plunges me into lived experience, particularity: I see scars, disfigurements, discolorations, damages, losses, as well as what pleases me. Bones well nourished from the placenta; the teeth of a middle-class person seen by the dentist twice a year from childhood. White skin, marked and scarred by three pregnancies, an elected sterilization, progressive arthritis, four joint operations, calcium deposits, no rapes, no abortions, long hours at a typewriter—my own, not in a typing pool—and so forth. To say "the body" lifts me away from what has given me a primary perspective. To say "my body" reduces the temptation to grandiose assertions.

This body. White, female; or female, white. The first obvious, lifelong facts. But I was born in the white section of a hospital that separated Black and white women in labor and Black and white babies in the nursery, just as it separated Black and white bodies in its morgue. I was defined as white before I was defined as female.

The politics of location. Even to begin with my body I have to say that from the outset that body had more than one identity. When I was carried out of the hospital into the world, I was viewed and treated as female, but also viewed and treated as white—by both Black and white people. I was located by color and sex as surely as a Black child was located by color and sex—though the implications of white identity were mystified by the presumption that white people are the center of the universe.

To locate myself in my body means more than understanding what it has meant to me to have a vulva and clitoris and uterus and breasts. It means recognizing this white skin, the places it has taken me, the places it has not let me go.

The body I was born into was not only female and white, but Jewish—enough for geographic location to have played, in those years, a determining part. I was a *Mischling*, four years old when the Third Reich began. Had it been not Baltimore, but Prague or Łódź or Amsterdam, the ten-year-old letter writer might have had no address. Had I survived Prague, Amsterdam, or Łódź and the railway stations for which they were deportation points, I would be some body else. My center, perhaps, the Middle East or Latin America, my language itself another language. Or I might be in no body at all.

But I am a North American Jew, born and raised three thousand miles from the war in Europe.

Trying as women to see from the center. "A politics," I wrote once, "of asking women's questions." We are not "the woman question" asked by somebody else; we are the women who ask the questions.

Trying to see so much, aware of so much to be seen, brought into the light, changed. Breaking down again and again the false male universal. Piling piece by piece of concrete experience side by side, comparing, beginning to discern patterns. Anger, frustration with Marxist or Leftist dismissals of these questions, this struggle. Easy now to call this disillusionment facile, but the anger was deep, the frustration real, both in personal relationships and political organizations. I wrote in 1975: *Much of what is narrowly termed "politics" seems to rest on a longing for certainty even at the cost of hon-esty, for an analysis which, once given, need not be reexamined. Such is the deadendedness—for women—of Marxism in our time.*

And it has felt like a dead end wherever politics has been ex-ternalized, cut off from the ongoing lives of women or of men, rarefied into an elite jargon, an enclave, defined by little sects who feed off each others' errors.

But even as we shrugged away Marx along with the acade-mic Marxists and the sectarian Left, some of us, calling our-selves radical feminists, never meant anything less by women's liberation than the creation of a society without domination; we never meant less than the making new of all relationships. The problem was that we did not know whom we meant when we said "we."

The power men everywhere wield over women, power which has become a model for every other form of exploitation and il-legitimate control. I wrote these words in 1978 at the end of an essay called "Compulsory Heterosexuality and Lesbian Ex-istence." Patriarchy as the "model" for other forms of domi-nation—this idea was not original with me. It has been put forward insistently by white Western feminists, and in 1972 I had quoted from Lévi-Strauss: *I would go so far as to say that even before slavery or class domination existed, men built an ap-proach to women that would serve one day to introduce differ-ences among us all.*

Living for fifty-some years, having watched even minor bits of history unfold, I am less quick than I once was to search for single "causes" or origins in dealings among human beings. But suppose that we could trace back and establish that pa-triarchy has been everywhere the model. To what choices of action does that lead us in the present? Patriarchy exists nowhere in a pure state; we are the latest to set foot in a tangle of oppressions grown up and around each other for centuries. This isn't the old children's game where you choose one strand of color in the web and follow it back to find your prize, ignoring the others as mere distractions. The prize is life itself, and most women in the world must fight for their lives on many fronts at once.

We . . . often find it difficult to separate race from class from sex oppression because in our lives they are most often experienced simultaneously. We know that there is such a thing as racial-sexual oppression which is neither solely racial nor solely sexual. . . . We need to articulate the real class situation of persons who are not merely raceless, sexless workers but for whom racial and sexual oppression are significant determinants in their working/economic lives.

This is from the 1977 Combahee River Collective statement, a major document of the U.S. women's movement, which gives a clear and uncompromising Black-feminist naming to the experience of simultaneity of oppressions.

Even in the struggle against free-floating abstraction, we have abstracted. Marxists and radical feminists have both done this. Why not admit it, get it said, so we can get on to the work to be done, back down to earth again? The faceless, sexless, raceless proletariat. The faceless, raceless, classless category of "all women." Both creations of white Western self-centeredness.

To come to terms with the circumscribing nature of (our) whiteness. Marginalized though we have been as women, as white and Western makers of theory, we also marginalize others because our lived experience is thoughtlessly white, because even our "women's cultures" are rooted in some Western tradition. Recognizing our location, having to name the ground we're coming from, the conditions we have taken for granted—there is a confusion between our claims to the white and Western eye and the woman-seeing eye, fear of losing the centrality of the one even as we claim the other.

How does the white Western feminist define theory? Is it something made only by white women and only by women acknowledged as writers? How does the white Western feminist define "an idea"? How do we actively work to build a white Western feminist consciousness that is not simply centered on itself, that resists white circumscribing?

It was in the writings but also the actions and speeches and sermons of Black United States citizens that I began to experience the meaning of my whiteness as a point of location for which I needed to take responsibility. It was in reading poems by contemporary Cuban women that I began to experience the meaning of North America as a location that had also shaped my ways of seeing and my ideas of who and what was important, a location for which I was also responsible. I traveled then to Nicaragua, where, in a tiny, impoverished country, in a four-year-old society dedicated to eradicating poverty, under the hills of the Nicaragua-Honduras border, I could physically feel the weight of the United States of North America, its military forces, its vast appropriations of money, its mass media, at my back; I could feel what it means, dissident or not, to be part of that raised boot of power, the cold shadow we cast everywhere to the south.

I come from a country stuck fast for forty years in the deep-freeze of history. Any United States citizen alive today has been saturated with Cold War rhetoric, the horrors of communism, the betrayals of socialism, the warning that any collective restructuring of society spells the end of personal freedom. And, yes, there have been horrors and betrayals deserving open opposition. But we are not invited to consider the butcheries of Stalinism, the terrors of the Russian counter-revolution alongside the butcheries of white supremacism and Manifest Destiny. We are not urged to help create a more human society here in response to the ones we are taught to hate and dread. Discourse itself is frozen at this level. Tonight as I turned a switch searching for "the news," that shinily animated silicone mask was on television again, telling the citizens of my country we are menaced by communism from El Salvador, that communism—Soviet variety, obviously—is on the move in Central America, that freedom is imperiled, that the suffering peasants of Latin America must be stopped, just as Hitler had to be stopped.

The discourse has never really changed; it is wearingly abstract. (Lillian Smith, white Southern anti-racist writer and activist, spoke of the "deadly sameness" of abstraction.) It allows no differences among places, times, cultures, conditions, movements. Words that should possess a depth and breadth of allusions—words like *socialism, communism, democracy, collectivism*—are stripped of their historical roots, the many faces of the struggles for social justice and independence reduced to an ambition to dominate the world.

Is there a connection between this state of mind—the Cold

War mentality, the attribution of all our problems to an external enemy—and a form of feminism so focused on male evil and female victimization that it, too, allows for no differences among women, men, places, times, cultures, conditions, classes, movements? Living in the climate of an enormous either/or, we absorb some of it unless we actively take heed.

In the United States large numbers of people have been cut off from their own process and movement. We have been hearing for forty years that we are the guardians of freedom, while "behind the Iron Curtain" all is duplicity and manipulation, if not sheer terror. Yet the legacy of fear lingering after the witch hunts of the fifties hangs on like the aftersmell of a burning. The sense of obliquity, mystery, paranoia surrounding the American Communist party after the Khrushchev Report of 1956: the party lost 30,000 members within weeks, and few who remained were talking about it. To be a Jew, a homosexual, any kind of marginal person was to be liable for suspicion of being "Communist." A blanketing snow had begun to drift over the radical history of the United States.

And, though parts of the North American feminist movement actually sprang from the Black movements of the sixties and the student Left, feminists have suffered not only from the burying and distortion of women's experience, but from the overall burying and distortion of the great movements for social change.

The first American woman astronaut is interviewed by the liberal-feminist editor of a mass-circulation women's magazine. She is a splendid creature, healthy, young, thick dark head of hair, scientific degrees from an elite university, an athletic self-confidence. She is also white. She speaks of the future of space, the potential uses of space colonies by private industry, especially for producing materials that can be advantageously processed under conditions of weightlessness. Pharmaceuticals, for example. By extension one thinks of chemicals. Neither of these two spirited women speak of the alliances between the military and the "private" sector of the North American economy. Nor do they speak of Depo-Provera, Valium, Librium, napalm, dioxin. *When big companies decide that it's now to their advantage to put a lot of their money into production of materials in space . . . we'll really get the funding that we need,* says the astronaut. No mention of who "we" are and what "we" need funding for; no questions about the poisoning and impoverishment of women here on earth or of the earth itself. Women, too, may leave the earth behind.

The astronaut is young, feels her own power, works hard for her exhilaration. She has swung out over the earth and come back, one more time passed all the tests. It's not that I expect her to come back to earth as Cassandra. But this experience of hers has nothing as yet to do with the liberation of women. A female proletariat—uneducated, ill nourished, unorganized, and largely from the Third World—will create the profits that will stimulate the "big companies" to invest in space.

On a split screen in my brain I see two versions of her story: the backward gaze through streaming weightlessness to the familiar globe, pale blue and green and white, the strict and sober presence of it, the true intuition of relativity battering the heart;

and the swiftly calculated move to a farther suburb, the male technocrats and the women they have picked and tested, leaving the familiar globe behind: the toxic rivers, the cancerous wells, the strangled valleys, the closed-down urban hospitals, the shattered schools, the atomic desert blooming, the lilac suckers run wild, the blue grape hyacinths spreading, the ailanthus and kudzu doing their final desperate part—the beauty that won't travel, that can't be stolen away.

A movement for change lives in feelings, actions, and words. Whatever circumscribes or mutilates our feelings makes it more difficult to act, keeps our actions reactive, repetitive: abstract thinking, narrow tribal loyalties, every kind of self-righteousness, the arrogance of believing ourselves at the center. It's hard to look back on the limits of my understanding a year, five years ago—how did I look without seeing, hear without listening? It can be difficult to be generous to earlier selves, and keeping faith with the continuity of our journeys is especially hard in the United States, where identities and loyalties have been shed and replaced without a tremor, all in the name of becoming "American." Yet how, except through ourselves, do we discover what moves other people to change? Our old fears and denials—what helps us let go of them? What makes us decide we have to re-educate ourselves, even those of us with "good" educations? A politicized life ought to sharpen both the senses and the memory.

The difficulty of saying I—a phrase from the East German novelist Christa Wolf. But once having said it, as we realize the necessity to go further, isn't there a difficulty of saying "we"? *You cannot speak for me. I cannot speak for us.* Two thoughts: there is no liberation that only knows how to say "I"; there is no collective movement that speaks for each of us all the way through.

And so even ordinary pronouns become a political problem.

- 64 cruise missiles in Greenham Common and Molesworth.
- 112 at Comiso.
- 96 Pershing II missiles in West Germany.
- 96 for Belgium and the Netherlands.

That is the projection for the next few years.

- Thousands of women, in Europe and the United States, saying *no* to this and to the militarization of the world.

An approach which traces militarism back to patriarchy and patriarchy back to the fundamental quality of maleness can be demoralizing and even paralyzing. . . . Perhaps it is possible to be less fixed on the discovery of "original causes." It might be more useful to ask, How do these values and behaviors get repeated generation after generation?

The valorization of manliness and masculinity. The armed forces as the extreme embodiment of the patriarchal family. The archaic idea of women as a "home front" even as the missiles are deployed in the backyards of Wyoming and Mutlangen. The growing urgency that an anti-nuclear, anti-militarist movement must be a feminist movement, must be a socialist movement, must be an anti-racist, anti-imperialist movement. That it's not enough to fear for the people we know, our own kind, ourselves. Nor is it empowering to give ourselves up to abstract terrors of pure annihilation. The anti-nuclear, anti-military movement cannot sweep away the missiles as a movement to save white civilization in the West.

The movement for change is a changing movement, changing itself, demasculinizing itself, de-Westernizing itself, becoming a critical mass that is saying in so many different voices, languages, gestures, actions: *It must change; we ourselves can change it.*

We who are not the same. We who are many and do not want to be the same.

————————

Trying to watch myself in the process of writing this, I keep coming back to something Sheila Rowbotham, the British socialist feminist, wrote:

> *A movement helps you to overcome some of the oppressive distancing of theory and this has been a . . . continuing creative endeavour of women's liberation. But some paths are not mapped and our footholds vanish. . . . I see what I'm writing as part of a wider claiming which is beginning. I am part of the difficulty myself. The difficulty is not out there.*

My difficulties, too, are not out there—except in the social conditions that make all this necessary. I do not any longer *believe*—my feelings do not allow me to believe—that the white eye sees from the center. Yet I often find myself thinking as if I still believed that were true. Or, rather, my thinking stands still. I feel in a state of arrest, as if my brain and heart were refusing to speak to each other. My brain, a woman's brain, has exulted in breaking the taboo against women thinking, has taken off on the wind, saying, *I am the woman who asks the questions.* My heart has been learning in a much more humble and laborious way, learning that feelings are useless without facts, that all privilege is ignorant at the core.

————————

The United States has never been a white country, though it has long served what white men defined as their interests. The Mediterranean was never white. England, northern Europe, if ever absolutely white, are so no longer. In a Leftist bookstore in Manchester, England, a Third World poster: *WE ARE HERE BECAUSE YOU WERE THERE.* In Europe there have always been the Jews, the original ghetto dwellers, identified as a racial type, suffering under pass laws and special entry taxes, enforced relocations, massacres: the scapegoats, the aliens, never seen as truly European but as part of that darker world that must be controlled, eventually exterminated. Today the cities of Europe have new scapegoats as well: the diaspora from the old colonial empires. Is anti-Semitism the model for racism, or racism for anti-Semitism? Once more, where does the question lead us? Don't we have to start here, where we are, forty years after the Holocaust, in the churn of Middle Eastern violence, in the midst of decisive ferment in South Africa—not in some debate over origins and precedents, but in the recognition of simultaneous oppressions?

———————

I've been thinking a lot about the obsession with origins. It seems a way of stopping time in its tracks. The sacred Neolithic triangles, the Minoan vases with staring eyes and breasts, the female figurines of Anatolia—weren't they concrete evidence of a kind, like Sappho's fragments, for earlier woman-affirming cultures, cultures that enjoyed centuries of peace? But haven't they also served as arresting images, which kept us attached and immobilized? Human activity didn't stop in Crete or Çatal Hüyük. We can't build a society free from domination by fixing our sights backward on some long-ago tribe or city.

The continuing spiritual power of an image lives in the interplay between what it reminds us of—what it *brings to mind*—and our own continuing actions in the present. When the labrys becomes a badge for a cult of Minoan goddesses, when the wearer of the labrys has ceased to ask herself what she is doing on this earth, where her love of women is taking her, the labrys, too, becomes abstraction—lifted away from the heat and friction of human activity. The Jewish star on my neck must serve me both for reminder and as a goad to continuing and changing responsibility.

When I learn that in 1913, mass women's marches were held in South Africa which caused the rescinding of entry permit laws; that in 1956, 20,000 women assembled in Pretoria to protest pass laws for women, that resistance to these laws was carried out in remote country villages and punished by shootings, beatings, and burnings; that in 1959, 2,000 women demonstrated in Durban against laws that provided beerhalls for African men and criminalized women's traditional home brewing; that at one and the same time, African women have played a major role alongside men in resisting apartheid, I have to ask myself why it took me so long to learn these chapters of women's history, why the leadership and strategies of African women have been so unrecognized as theory in action by white Western feminist thought. (And in a book by two men, entitled *South African Politics* and published in 1982, there is one entry under "Women" [franchise] and no reference anywhere to women's political leadership and mass actions.)

When I read that a major strand in the conflicts of the past decade in Lebanon has been political organizing by women of women, across class and tribal and religious lines, women working and teaching together within refugee camps and armed communities, and of the violent undermining of their efforts through the civil war and the Israeli invasion, I am forced to think. Iman Khalife, the young teacher who tried to organize a silent peace march on the Christian-Moslem border of Beirut—a protest that was quelled by the threat of a massacre of the participants—Iman Khalife and women like her do not come out of nowhere. But Western feminists, living under other kinds of conditions, are not encouraged to know this background.

And I turn to Etel Adnan's brief, extraordinary novel *Sitt Marie Rose*, about a middle-class Christian Lebanese woman tortured for joining the Palestinian Resistance, and read:

> **She was also subject to another great delusion believing that women are protected from repression, and that the leaders considered political fights to be strictly between males. In fact, with women's greater access to certain powers, they began to watch them more closely, and perhaps with even greater hostility. Every feminine act, even charitable and seemingly unpolitical ones, were regarded as a rebellion in this world where women had always played servile roles. Marie Rose inspired scorn and hate long before the fateful day of her arrest.**

Across the curve of the earth, there are women getting up before dawn, in the blackness before the point of light, in the twilight before sunrise; there are women rising earlier than men and children to break the ice, to start the stove, to put up the pap, the coffee, the rice, to iron the pants, to braid the hair, to pull the day's water up from the well, to boil water for tea, to wash the children for school, to pull the vegetables and start the walk to market, to run to catch the bus for the work that is paid. I don't know when most women sleep. In big cities at dawn women are traveling home after cleaning offices all night, or waxing the halls of hospitals, or sitting up with the old and sick and frightened at the hour when death is supposed to do its work.

In Peru: "Women invest hours in cleaning tiny stones and chaff out of beans, wheat and rice; they shell peas and clean fish and grind spices in small mortars. They buy bones or tripe at the market and cook cheap, nutritious soups. They repair clothes until they will not sustain another patch. They . . . search . . . out the cheapest school uniforms, payable in the greatest number of installments. They trade old magazines for plastic washbasins and buy secondhand toys and shoes. They walk long distances to find a spool of thread at a slightly lower price."

This is the working day that has never changed, the unpaid female labor that means the survival of the poor.

In minimal light I see her, over and over, her inner clock pushing her out of bed with her heavy 'and maybe painful limbs, her breath breathing life into her stove, her house, her family, taking the last cold swatch of night on her body, meeting the sudden leap of the rising sun.

In my white North American world they have tried to tell me that this woman—politicized by intersecting forces—doesn't think and reflect on her life. That her ideas are not real ideas like those of Karl Marx and Simone de Beauvoir. That her calculations, her spiritual philosophy, her gifts for law and ethics, her daily emergency political decisions are merely instinctual or conditioned reactions. That only certain kinds of people can make theory; that the white-educated mind is capable of formulating everything; that white middle-class feminism can know for "all women"; that only when a white mind formulates is the formulation to be taken seriously.

In the United States, white-centered theory has not yet adequately engaged with the texts—written, printed, and widely available—that have been for a decade or more formulating the political theory of black American feminism: the Combahee River Collective statement, the essays and speeches of

Gloria I. Joseph, Audre Lorde, Bernice Reagon, Michele Russell, Barbara Smith, June Jordan, to name a few of the most obvious. White feminists have read and taught from the anthology *This Bridge Called My Back: Writings by Radical Women of Color*, yet often have perceived it simply as an angry attack on the white women's movement. So white feelings remain at the center. And, yes, I need to move outward from the base and center of my feelings, but with a corrective sense that my feelings are not *the* center of feminism.

And if we read Audre Lorde or Gloria Joseph or Barbara Smith, do we understand that the intellectual roots of this feminist theory are not white liberalism or white Euro-American feminism, but the analyses of Afro-American experience articulated by Sojourner Truth, W. E. B. Du Bois, Ida B. Wells-Barnett, C. L. R. James, Malcolm X, Lorraine Hansberry, Fannie Lou Hamer, among others? That Black feminism cannot be marginalized and circumscribed as simply a response to white feminist racism or an augmentation of white feminism; that it is an organic development of the Black movements and philosophies of the past, their practice and their printed writings? (And that, increasingly, Black American feminism is actively in dialogue with other movements of women of color within and beyond the United States?)

To shrink from or dismiss that challenge can only isolate white feminism from the other great movements for self-determination and justice within and against which women define ourselves.

Once again: Who is *we?*

This is the end of these notes, but it is not an ending.

1984

Raya Dunayevskaya's Marx

This essay first appeared as the foreword to the second edition of Raya Dunayevskaya's Rosa Luxemburg, Women's Liberation and Marx's Philosophy of Revolution *(Champaign-Urbana: University of Illinois Press, 1991). I had previously written a review-essay on Dunayevskaya's work when the first edition of* Women's Liberation and the Dialectics of Revolution *was published in 1985 (See* The Women's Review of Books 3, *no. 12 (September 1986): 1, 3–4.*

Raya Dunayevskaya was a major thinker in the history of Marxism and of women's liberation—one of the longest continuously active woman revolutionaries of the twentieth century. In fierce intellectual and political independence, her life and work defied many mind-numbing labels that self-described conservatives, liberals, and radicals have applied to voices for political and social change. Born in 1910, between two revolutions, she said of her beginnings:

> **I come from Russia 1917, and the ghettos of Chicago, where I first saw a Black person. The reason that I'm starting that way—it happens to be true—but the reason that I'm starting that way is that I was illiterate. You know, you're born in a border town—there's a revolution, there's a counter-**

revolution, there's anti-Semitism—you *know* nothing, but experience a lot. . . . That is, you don't know that you're a revolutionary, but you're opposed to everything.

Now, how does it happen that an illiterate person, who certainly didn't know Lenin and Trotsky, who as a child had never seen a Black, had begun to develop all the revolutionary ideas to be called Marxist-Humanism in the 1950's? It isn't personal whatsoever! If you live when an idea is born, and a great revolution in the world is born—it doesn't make any difference *where* you are; *that becomes the next stage of development of humanity.*

Dunayevskaya was using her own early life to illustrate a core theme of her writing: the inseparability of experience and revolutionary thinking, the falseness of the opposition between "philosophy" and "actuality." Her readings of past history and contemporary politics were drenched in the conviction that while thinking and action are not the same, they must continually readdress and renew each other. For the spontaneous responses of a Russian Jewish girl, growing up in a climate of revolution, brought at the age of twelve to the Jewish ghetto in Chicago (in the twenties she "moved herself" to the black ghetto), to become the ongoing catalyst for a lifetime's commitment to human freedom, required a structuring of her experience that Marx's (not Marx*ist*) theory was soon to provide her. She was to become not just literate, but learned in philosophy and history—and here again labels fail us, since for Dunayevskaya philosophy *was* the making of history: the envisioning of "the day after," "the creation of a new society." At the same time, her political activities—first among black activists, then with the West Virginia miners' strike of 1949–50, and so on into the Women's Liberation Movement of the past two decades—set her on a lifelong path of both participating in and reflecting on mass movements.

The separation—willed or unaware—of intellectuals from the people they theorize about, the estrangement of self-styled vanguards and their "correct lines" from actual people's needs and aspirations, is hardly news. Dunayevskaya tried, in the very structure of her life and writings, to show us a different method. What does it look like when, as part of a movement, we try to think *along with* the human forces newly pushing forth, in ever-changing forms and with ever-different faces? How can we conceptualize a miners' strike, a poor people's march, a ghetto revolt, a women's demonstration *both* as "spontaneous activity" *and* as the embodiment of new ideas— not yet perhaps written down except in rain-blurred flyers— about power, resources, control of the products of one's labor, the ability to live humanly among other humans? How do we extract new kinds of "reason" or "idea" from the activities of "new passions and new forces" (Marx's phrase) without losing continuity with past struggles for freedom? How do we think clearly in times of great turmoil, revolution, or counterrevolution without resorting to a party line based only on past dogma or on internecine graspings for power? How do we create a philosophy of revolution that itself helps make revolution possible? The American Communist party was to lose its way among such questions.

Dunayevskaya's way of grounding herself was to turn to Marx. Not, I should emphasize, as a *turning backward* but as rescuing for the present a legacy she saw as still unclaimed, having been diminished, distorted, and betrayed by post-Marx Marxists and the emerging "Communist" states. But she didn't simply turn to Marx, or to Hegel (whose work she saw as a living, still uncomprehended, presence in Marx's own thought), as texts. Her work, including *Rosa Luxemburg,* is an explication of the fullness of Marx's thought *as she came to live it,* in living through the liberation movements of her own era. She translated Marx, interpreted Marx, fitted together fragments of Marx scattered in post-Marxist schisms, refused to leave Marx enshrined as dead text, ill read, or relegated to "the dustbin of history."

It was Marx's humanism above all that she felt had never been adequately understood—in particular his recognition of what she called the black and women's dimensions, but more largely as he sought not merely the "overthrow" of capitalism but a vision of "revolution in permanence," a dynamically unfolding society in which the human individual could freely develop and express her or his creativity; not a static Communist utopia but an evolving human community.

I come out of a strain of feminism that saw itself as a leap forward out of Marxism, leaving the male Left behind, and for which a term like *Marxist-Humanism* would, in the late sixties and early seventies, have sounded like a funeral knell. A major problem (a problem not just of language but of organizing) was to break from a paradigm of class struggle that erased women's labor except in the paid workplace (often even there), and also from a "humanist" false universal deriving from the European Renaissance glorification of the male. Radical feminists were of necessity concerned with keeping the political focus on women because in every other focus—race, class, nation—women had gotten lost, put down, marginalized. In addition, we were fighting a dogma of class as the primary oppression, capitalism as the single source of all oppressions. We insisted that women were, if not a class, a caste; if not a caste, an oppressed group *as women*—*within* oppressed groups *and* within the middle and ruling classes.

And, as Dunayevskaya is quick to point out, "the Women's Liberation Movement that burst onto the historic scene in the mid-1960s was like nothing seen before in all its many appearances throughout history. Its most unique feature was that, surprisingly, not only did it come out of the left but it was *directed against it,* and not from the right, but *from within the left itself.*" It's clear how eagerly she welcomed this new force as it sent shock waves through radical group after radical group, starting with the Student Nonviolent Coordinating Committee in 1965. But although her own thinking was obviously incited and nourished by the contemporary Women's Liberation Movement, she had, even in the forties, recognized "the woman dimension," and one of her earliest essays in *Women's Liberation and the Dialectics of Revolution* is an account of organizing by miners' wives in the 1949–50 anti-automation strikes in West Virginia. Dunayevskaya recognized women not just as revolutionary "Force" (contributing courage, support, strength) but also as "Reason"—as initiators, thinkers, strategists, creators of the new.

The first thing to strike a reader, ranging through Dunayevskaya's books, is the vitality, combativeness, relish, impatience of her voice. Hers is not the prose of a disembodied intellectual. She argues; she challenges; she urges on; she expostulates; her essays have the spontaneity of an extemporaneous speech (some of them are) or of a notebook—you can hear her thinking aloud. She has a prevailing sense of ideas as flesh and blood, of the individual thinker, limited by her or his individuality yet carrying on a conversation in the world. The thought of the philosopher is a product of what she or he has lived through.

Marxism and Freedom (1957) is a history of the process of Marx's thought, as it evolved out of eighteenth-century philosophy and Hegel's dialectic through the mass political movements of the nineteenth century, as it became adapted and modified by Engels, Trotsky, and Lenin and, finally, in Dunayevskaya's words, "totally perverted" by Stalin. She traced the shift from Marx's idea of a workers' state with no separation of manual and mental labor, to Lenin's failed attempt to create a "workers' state," to Stalin's creation of a corporate totalitarian state run by the Communist party—which she defines as counterrevolution. She saw, in the East German workers' strike of 1953 and the Hungarian Revolution of 1956, evidence of a continuing revolutionary spirit in Eastern Europe (which was to capture world attention in the upheavals of 1989). She ends the first edition of *Marxism and Freedom* with the Montgomery bus boycott as a spontaneous movement kept within the hands of black people.

In *Marxism and Freedom,* Dunayevskaya grapples, in the face of the Stalinist legacy, with the question: *What happens after?* What happens when the old oppression has been successfully resisted and overthrown? What turns revolutionary leaders into tyrants? Why did the Russian revolution turn backward on itself? How do we make the "continuing revolution" "the revolution in permanence" in which this cannot happen? She is passionate about "the movement from theory to practice and from practice to theory" as a living process and about the necessity for new voices speaking for their own freedom to be heard and listened to, if a movement is to keep on moving. She had the capacity, rare in people learned in Western philosophy and theory—including Marxists—to respect and learn from other kinds of thinking and other modes of expression: those of the Third World, of ordinary militant women, of working people who are perfectly aware that theirs is "alienated labor" and know how to say that without political indoctrination. Maybe Dunayevskaya would claim she originally learned this from Marx.

Marxism and Freedom has as its focus the "movement from practice to theory." Dunayevskaya writes of the shaping impact of American slavery and the Civil War on Marx's thought when he was writing *Capital;* she acknowledges the unfinished legacy of Reconstruction and recognizes the acute significance of the Montgomery bus boycott—the "Black dimension." Women's liberation is not yet a focus, although already in the fifties, long before *Marxism and Freedom* was written, Dunayevskaya was keenly attuned to women's leadership and presence both within and outside radical groups. In "The Miners' Wives" (1950) she notes that while the press depicted the women as bravely going along with the strike, they were in fact activists, sometimes pushing the men. In a long-unpublished essay of 1953, she sharply criticizes the Socialist Workers party for failing to recognize that the women who had streamed by the millions into factories in the United States during World War II were "a concrete revolutionary force" searching for "a total reorganization of society." "By continuing her [*sic*] revolt daily at home, the women were giving a new dimension to politics" (*Women's Liberation and the Dialectics of Revolution*, p. 34). Perhaps it's not by mere oversight that this essay remained so long unpublished. In it Dunayevskaya makes clear that the equality of some women as leaders within the party did not extend to any real recognition of women as a major social force. Possibly her own consciousness of women, though keen, received only negative responses in the organization of which she was then a part. But her entire life was a demonstration of "Woman as Force and Reason," activist and thinker.

Philosophy and Revolution (1973) retraces some of the history of philosophy in *Marxism and Freedom,* moving on from there to discuss the Cuban revolution and the student and youth uprisings of the sixties, along with the emergence of the Women's Liberation Movement. This work feels—until the last chapter—less dynamic and more laborious, more like a political-philosophy textbook. But in both books, Dunayevskaya is on a very specific mission: to rescue

Marx's Marxism from the theoretical and organizational systems attributed to him; to reclaim his ideas from what has been served up as Marxism in Eastern Europe, China, Cuba, and among Western intellectuals. She insists that you cannot sever Marx's economics from his humanism—humanism here meaning the self-emancipation of human beings necessarily from the capitalist mode of production, but not only from that. The failure of the Russian revolutions to continue as "revolution in permanence"—their disintegration into a system of forced labor camps and political prisons—was the shock that sent Dunayevskaya back to "the original form of the Humanism of Marx," translating his early humanist essays herself because "the official Moscow publication (1959) is marred by footnotes which flagrantly violate Marx's content and intent." "Marxism is a theory of liberation or it is nothing." But she refuses to "rebury" Marx as "humanist," shorn of his economics.

Rosa Luxemburg (1982) is much more than a philosophical biography. But that it certainly is: a sympathetic yet critical account of Luxemburg as woman, thinker, organizer, revolutionist. A central chapter is devoted to Marx and Luxemburg as theorists of capital, dissecting Luxemburg's critique of Marx in her *Accumulation of Capital*. Dunayevskaya dissents at many points from Luxemburg's effort to fulfill, as she saw it, Marx's unfinished work. But beyond the economic debate Dunayevskaya asserts that Luxemburg, despite her eloquent writings on imperialism, never saw the potential for revolution in the colonized people of color in what is now called the Third World; and, despite the centrality of women to her antimilitarist work, never saw beyond the purely economic class struggle. Where Marx had seen "new forces and new passions spring up in the bosom of society" as capitalism declined, Luxemburg saw only the "suffering masses" under imperialism.

Luxemburg was "a reluctant feminist" who was "galled in a most personal form" by the "Woman Question" but, "just as she had learned to live with an underlying anti-Semitism in the party, so she learned to live with . . . male chauvinism." (Does this have a familiar ring?) In particular, she lived with it in the figure of August Bebel, a self-proclaimed feminist who wrote of her "wretched female's squirts of poison," and Viktor Adler, who called her "the poisonous bitch . . . clever as a monkey." However, when she was arrested in 1915 it was on the eve of organizing an international women's antiwar conference with Clara Zetkin. Of their relationship Dunayevskaya says: "Far from Luxemburg having no interest in the so-called 'Woman Question,' and far from Zetkin having no interest outside of that question, . . . both of them . . . were determined to build a women's liberation movement that concentrated not only on organizing women workers but on having them develop as leaders, as decision-makers, and as independent Marxist revolutionaries." In fact, from 1902 on Luxemburg had been writing and speaking on the emancipation of women and on woman suffrage; in 1911 she wrote to her friend Louise Kautsky, "Are you coming for the women's conference? Just imagine, I have become a feminist!" She debated Bebel and Kautsky over the "Woman Question," and broke with Kautsky in 1911, yet, in her short and brutally ended life, feminism and proletarian revolution never became integrated. Dunayevskaya is critical of Luxemburg but also impatient with present-day feminists who want to write her off.

In Luxemburg, Dunayevskaya portrays a brilliant, brave, and independent woman, passionately internationalist and antiwar, a believer in the people's "spontaneity" in the cause of freedom; a woman who saw herself as Marx's philosophical heir, who refused the efforts of her lover and other men to discourage her from full participation in "making history" because she was a woman. But the biography does not stop here. The book opens into a structure generated, as Dunayevskaya tells us, by three events: the resurgence of the Women's Liberation Movement out of the Left; the publication for the first time of Marx's last writings, the *Ethnological Notebooks;* and the global national liberation movements of the seventies that demonstrated to her that Marxism continues to have meaning as a philosophy of revolution. Luxemburg's life and thought become a kind of jumping-off point into the present and future—what she saw and didn't see, her limitations as well as her understanding. We can learn from her mistakes, says Dunayevskaya, as she begins developing the themes she would pursue in *Women's Liberation and the Dialectics of Revolution.*

In this thirty-five-year collection of essays, interviews, letters, lectures you see Dunayevskaya going at her central ideas in many different ways. Agree or not with her analysis here, her interpretation there: these working papers are some of the most tingling, invigorating writing since the early days of Women's Liberation when writing and organizing most often went hand in hand. In her irresistible depiction of women in movement, across the world and through history, Dunayevskaya really does hold to an international perspective. She chides and criticizes Simone de Beauvoir, Sheila Rowbotham, Gerda Lerner; she praises *Wuthering Heights, A Room of One's Own,* the "Three Marias" of the *New Portuguese Letters,* the poetry of Gwendolyn Brooks and Audre Lorde; she says Natalia Trotsky went further than Trotsky; she chastises Engels for diluting and distorting Marx, and post-Marxists and feminists for accepting Engels's *Origins of the Family* as *Marx's* word on women and men. Her quarrel with the Western post-Marxists is that they've taken parts of Marx for the whole, and that what has been left out (especially the dimensions of women and the Third World) is crucial in our time. Her quarrel with the Women's Movement is that feminists have jettisoned Marx because he was a man, or have believed the post-Marxists without looking into Marx for themselves. She insists that Marx's philosophy, far from being a closed and autocratic system, is open-ended, so that "in each age, he becomes more alive than in the age before." That Marx was himself extraordinarily open to other voices than those of European males.

But why do we need Marx, anyway? Dunayevskaya believes he is the only philosopher of "total revolution"—the revolution that will touch and transform all human relationships, that is never-ending, revolution in permanence. Permanence not as a party-led state that has found all the answers, but as a society all of whose people participate in both government and production and in which the division between manual and mental labor will be ended. We need such a philosophy as grounding for organizing, since, as she says in *Rosa Luxemburg*, "without a philosophy of revolution activism spends itself in mere anti-imperialism and anti-capitalism, without ever revealing what it is *for*."

Dunayevskaya bases her claims for Marx on her reading of his entire work, but attaches special importance to the *Ethnological Notebooks* (only transcribed and published in 1972) as showing that at the very end of his life, as in his early writings, he was concerned with humanism—not simply class struggle but with the values and structures of precapitalist, non-European societies and the relationship of the sexes in those societies. In these manuscripts, jotted between 1881 and 1882, Marx reviewed the anthropological-ethnological writings of Lewis Henry Morgan (Engels based his *Origins* on Marx's notes on Morgan), John Budd Phear, Henry Maine, and John Lubbock. And indeed, as I read the *Notebooks*, Marx seems to be on a search for how gender has been structured in precapitalist, tribal societies.

Marx didn't go along with the ethnologists in their definitions of the "savage" as measured against the "civilized." Capitalism doesn't mean progress; the civilized are also the damaged. He saw "civilization" as a divided condition—human subjectivity divided against itself by the division of labor, but also divided *from* nature. He was critical of Morgan for ignoring white genocide and ethnocide against the American Indians, of Phear's condescension toward Bengali culture, and of the ethnocentricity of the ethnographers in general.

But neither did Marx idealize egalitarian communal society; he saw that "the elements of oppression in general, and of woman in particular, arose from *within* primitive communism, and not only related to change from 'matriarchy,' but began with the establishment of ranks—relationship of chief to mass—and the economic interests that accompanied it." He watched closely how the family evolved into an economic unit, within which were the seeds of slavery and serfdom, how tribal conflict and conquest also led toward slavery and the acquisition of property. But where Engels posited "the world historic defeat of the female sex," Dunayevskaya notes that Marx saw the resistance of the women in every revolution, not simply how they were disempowered by the development of patriarchy and by European invasion and colonization. The *Ethnological Notebooks* are crucial in Dunayevskaya's eyes because they show Marx at a point in his life where his idea of revolution was becoming even more comprehensive: the colonialism that evolved out of capitalism forced him to return to precolonial societies to study human relations and "to see the possibility of new human relations, not as they might come through a mere 'updating' of primitive communism's equality of the sexes . . . but as Marx sensed they would burst forth from a new type of revolution."

Dunayevskaya vehemently opposes the notion that Marx's Marxism means that class struggle is primary or that racism and male supremacism will end when capitalism falls. "What happens after?" she says, is the question we have to be asking all along. And this, she sees in the Women's Liberation Movement, both women of color and white women have insisted on asking.

And, indeed, what is finally so beautiful and compelling about the Marx she shows us is his resistance to all static, stagnant ways of being, the deep apprehension of motion and transformation as principles of thought and of human process, the mind-weaving dialectical shuttle aflight in the loom of human activity.

Raya Dunayevskaya caught fire from Marx, met it with her own fire, brought to the events of her lifetime a revitalized, re-focused Marxism. Her writings, with all their passion, energy, wit, and learning, may read awkwardly at times because she is really writing against the grain of how many readers have learned to think: to separate disciplines and genres, theory from practice. She's trying to think, and write, the revolution in the revolution. Anyone who has tried to do this, in any medium, knows that the effect is not smooth or seamless.

Rosa Luxemburg may not fit the expectations of many readers schooled in leftist, feminist, or academic thought. It is, first of all, not a conventional biography but rather the history and critique of a thinking woman's mind. It supplies no anecdotes of Luxemburg's childhood, no dramatic version of her assassination. It does, however, explore the question of how Luxemburg's sexual and political relationship with Leo Jogiches expressed itself both in intimate letters and in her theory. But Luxemburg's central relationships, in Dunayevskaya's eyes, were her intellectual relationship with the work of Marx as she understood it and the relationship of her whole self to the revolution. Most biographers of women still fail to recognize that a woman's central relationship can be to her work, even as lovers come and go. And Dunayevskaya doesn't end the book with Luxemburg's death, because she doesn't see that death as an ending. She goes on to throw out lines of thinking for the future, lines that pass through Luxemburg's fiery figure but don't finish with the woman who "joyfully [threw her] whole life 'on the scales of destiny.' "

"No one knows where the end of suffering will begin," writes Nadine Gordimer about the 1976 Soweto schoolchildren's uprising in her novel *Burger's Daughter*. In her 1982 essay "Living in the Interregnum," she muses about the sources of art and goes on, "It is from there, in the depths of being, that the most important intuition of revolutionary faith comes: the people know what to do, before the leaders."

Dunayevskaya concludes:

> It isn't because we are any "smarter" that we can see so much more than other post-Marx Marxists. Rather, it is because of the maturity of our age. It is true that other post-Marx Marxists have rested on a truncated Marxism; it is equally true that no other generation could have seen the problematic of our age, much less solve our problems. *Only live human beings can recreate the revolutionary dialectic forever anew* [emphasis mine]. And these live human beings must do so in theory as well as in practice. It is not a question only of meeting the challenge from practice, but of being able to meet the challenge from the self-development of the Idea, and of deepening theory to the point where it reaches Marx's concept of the philosophy of "revolution in permanence."

And this work is indeed going on. Chicana lesbian-feminist poet, activist, and theorist Gloria Anzaldúa writes, in 1990:

> What does being a thinking subject, an intellectual, mean for women-of-color from working-class origins? . . . It means

being concerned about the ways knowledges are invented. It means continually challenging institutionalized discourses. It means being suspicious of the dominant culture's interpretation of "our" experience, of the way they "read" us. . . .

. . . Theory produces effects that change people and the way they perceive the world. Thus we need *teorías* that will enable us to interpret what happens in the world, that will explain how and why we relate to certain people in specific ways, that will reflect what goes on between inner, outer and peripheral "I"s within a person and between the personal "I"s and the collective "we" of our ethnic communities. *Necesitamos teorías* that will rewrite history using race, class, gender and ethnicity as categories of analysis, theories that cross borders, that blur boundaries. . . . We need theories that point out ways to maneuver between our particular experiences and the necessity of forming our own categories and theoretical models for the patterns we uncover. . . . And we need to find practical applications for those theories. . . . We need to give up the notion that there is a "correct" way to write theory.

It's made so difficult, under the prevailing conditions of capital-shaped priorities, male supremacism, racism, militarism to envision that revolution without an end to which Dunayevskaya devoted her life. Most of us, even in our imaginations, settle for less. Living under these conditions, we can lose sight of the fact that *we* "live human beings" are where it all must begin—lose sight even to the point of denying the degree to which we are suffering. At certain moments, if we're lucky, we touch the experience, the flash, of *how it would feel to be free*. Raya Dunayevskaya clearly never let go of her experiences of the fullness of being human, of "how it would feel"—and she wanted that experience to be the normal experience of every human being everywhere.

1991

Why I Refused the National Medal for the Arts

After the text of my letter to Jane Alexander, then chair of the National Endowment for the Arts, had been fragmentarily quoted in various news stories, Steve Wasserman, editor of the Los Angeles Times Book Review, asked me for an article expanding on my reasons. Herewith the letter and the article.

July 3, 1997

Jane Alexander, Chair
The National Endowment for the Arts
1100 Pennsylvania Avenue
Washington, D.C. 20506

Dear Jane Alexander,

I just spoke with a young man from your office, who informed me that I had been chosen to be one of twelve recipients of the National Medal for the Arts at a ceremony at the White House in the fall. I told him at once that I could not accept such an award from President Clinton or this White House because the very meaning of art, as I understand it, is incompatible with the cynical politics of this administration. I want to clarify to you what I meant by my refusal.

Anyone familiar with my work from the early sixties on knows that I believe in art's social presence—as breaker of official silences, as voice for those whose voices are disregarded, and as a human birthright. In my lifetime I have seen the space for the arts opened by movements for social justice, the power of art to break despair. Over the past two decades I have witnessed the increasingly brutal impact of racial and economic injustice in our country.

There is no simple formula for the relationship of art to justice. But I do know that art—in my own case the art of poetry—means nothing if it simply decorates the dinner table of power that holds it hostage. The radical disparities of wealth and power in America are widening at a devastating rate. A president cannot meaningfully honor certain token artists while the people at large are so dishonored.

I know you have been engaged in a serious and disheartening struggle to save government funding for the arts, against those whose fear and suspicion of art is nakedly repressive. In the end, I don't think we can separate art from overall human dignity and hope. My concern for my country is inextricable from my concerns as an artist. I could not participate in a ritual that would feel so hypocritical to me.

Sincerely,
Adrienne Rich

cc: President Clinton

––––––––––––

The invitation from the White House came by telephone on July 3. After several years' erosion of arts funding and hostile propaganda from the religious right and the Republican Congress, the House vote to end the National Endowment for the Arts was looming. That vote would break as news on July 10;

my refusal of the National Medal for the Arts would run as a sidebar story alongside in the *New York Times* and the *San Francisco Chronicle*.

In fact, I was unaware of the timing. My refusal came directly out of my work as a poet and essayist and citizen drawn to the interfold of personal and public experience. I had recently been thinking and writing about the shrinking of the social compact, of whatever it was this country had ever meant when it called itself a democracy: the shredding of the vision of *government of the people, by the people, for the people*.

"We the people—still an excellent phrase," said the playwright Lorraine Hansberry in 1962, well aware who had been excluded, yet believing the phrase might someday come to embrace us all. And I had for years been feeling both personal and public grief, fear, hunger, and the need to render this, my time, in the language of my art.

Whatever was "newsworthy" about my refusal was not about a single individual—not myself, not President Clinton. Nor was it about a single political party. Both major parties have displayed a crude affinity for the interests of corporate power, while deserting the majority of the people, especially the most vulnerable. Like so many others, I've watched the dismantling of our public education, the steep rise in our incarceration rates, the demonization of our young black men, the accusations against our teen-age mothers, the selling of health care—public and private—to the highest bidders, the export of subsistence-level jobs in the United States to even lower-wage countries, the use of below-minimum-wage prison labor to break strikes and raise profits, the scapegoating of immigrants, the denial of dignity and minimal security to working and poor people. At the same time, we've witnessed the acquisition of publishing houses, once risk-taking conduits of creativity, by conglomerates driven single-mindedly to fast profits, the acquisition of major communications and media by those same interests, the sacrifice of the arts and public libraries in stripped-down school and civic budgets, and, most recently, the evisceration of the National Endowment for the Arts. Piece by piece the democratic process has been losing ground to the accumulation of private wealth.

There is no political leadership in the White House or the Congress that has spoken to and for the people who, in a very real sense, have felt abandoned by their government.

Lorraine Hansberry spoke her words about government during the Cuban missile crisis, at a public meeting in New York to abolish the House Un-American Activities Committee. She also said in that speech, "My government is wrong." She did not say, I abhor all government. She claimed her government as a citizen, African American, and female, and she challenged it. (I listened to her words again, on an old vinyl recording, this past Fourth of July.)

In a similar spirit many of us today might wish to hold government accountable, to challenge the agendas of private power and wealth that have displaced historical tendencies toward genuinely representative government in the United States. We might still wish to claim our government, to say, *This belongs to us*—we, the people, as we are now.

We would have to start asking questions that have been defined as nonquestions—or as naive, childish questions. In the recent official White House focus on race, it goes consistently unsaid that the all-embracing enterprise of our early history was the slave trade, which left nothing, no single life, untouched, and was, along with the genocide of the native population and the seizure of their lands, the foundation of our national prosperity and power. Promote dialogues on race? apologize for slavery? We would need to perform an autopsy on capitalism itself.

Marxism has been declared dead. Yet the questions Marx raised are still alive and pulsing, however the language and the labels have been co-opted and abused. What is social wealth? How do the conditions of human labor infiltrate other social relationships? What would it require for people to live and work together in conditions of radical equality? How much inequality will we tolerate in the world's richest and most powerful nation? Why and how have these and similar questions become discredited in public discourse?

And what about art? Mistrusted, adored, pietized, condemned, dismissed as entertainment, commodified, auctioned at Sotheby's, purchased by investment-seeking celebrities, it dies into the "art object" of a thousand museum basements. It's also reborn hourly in prisons, women's shelters, small-town garages, community-college workshops, halfway houses, wherever someone picks up a pencil, a wood-burning tool, a copy of *The Tempest,* a tag-sale camera, a whittling knife, a stick of charcoal, a pawnshop horn, a video of *Citizen Kane,* whatever lets you know again that this deeply instinctual yet self-conscious expressive language, this regenerative process, could help you save your life. "If there were no poetry on any day in the world," the poet Muriel Rukeyser wrote, "poetry would be invented that day. For there would be an intolerable hunger." In an essay on the Caribbean poet Aimé Césaire, Clayton Eshleman names this hunger as "the desire, the need, for a more profound and ensouled world." There is a continuing dynamic between art repressed and art reborn, between the relentless marketing of the superficial and the "spectral and vivid reality that employs all means" (Rukeyser again) to reach through armoring, resistances, resignation, to recall us to desire.

Art is both tough and fragile. It speaks of what we long to hear and what we dread to find. Its source and native impulse, the imagination, may be shackled in early life, yet may find release in conditions offering little else to the spirit. For a recent document on this, look at Phyllis Kornfeld's *Cellblock Visions: Prison Art in America,* notable for the variety and emotional depth of the artworks reproduced, the words of the inmate artists, and for Kornfeld's unsentimental and lucid text. Having taught art to inmates for fourteen years, in eighteen institutions (including maximum-security units), she sees recent incarceration policy as rapidly devolving from rehabilitation to dehumanization, including the dismantling of prison arts programs.

Art can never be totally legislated by any system, even those that reward obedience and send dissident artists to hard labor and death; nor can it, in our specifically compromised system, be really free. It may push up through cracked macadam, by the merest means, but it needs breathing space, cultivation, protection to fulfill itself. Just as people do. New artists, young or old, need education in their art, the tools of their craft, chances to study examples from the past and meet practitioners in the present, get the criticism and encouragement of mentors, learn that they are not alone. As the social compact withers, fewer and fewer people will be told *Yes, you can do this; this also belongs to you.* Like government, art needs the participation of the many in order not to become the property of a powerful and narrowly self-interested few.

Art is our human birthright, our most powerful means of access to our own and another's experience and imaginative life. In continually rediscovering and recovering the humanity of human beings, art is crucial to the democratic vision. A government tending further and further away from the search for democracy will see less and less "use" in encouraging artists, will see art as obscenity or hoax.

In 1987, the late Justice William Brennan spoke of "formal

reason severed from the insights of passion" as a major threat to due-process principles. "Due process asks whether government has treated someone fairly, whether individual dignity has been honored, whether the worth of an individual has been acknowledged. Officials cannot always silence these questions by pointing to rational action taken according to standard rules. They must plumb their conduct more deeply, seeking answers in the more complex equations of human nature and experience."

It is precisely where fear and hatred of art join the pull toward quantification and abstraction, where the human face is mechanically deleted, that human dignity disappears from the social equation. Because it is to those "complex equations of human nature and experience" that art addresses itself.

In a society tyrannized by the accumulation of wealth as Eastern Europe was tyrannized by its own false gods of concentrated power, recognized artists have, perhaps, a new opportunity: to work out our connectedness, *as artists,* with other people who are beleaguered, suffering, disenfranchised—precariously employed workers, trashed elders, rejected youth, the "unsuccessful," and the art they too are nonetheless making and seeking.

I wish I didn't feel the necessity to say here that none of this is about imposing ideology or style or content on artists; it's about the inseparability of art from acute social crisis in this century and the one now approaching.

We have a short-lived model, in our history, for the place of art in relation to government. During the Depression of the 1930s, under New Deal legislation, thousands of creative and performing artists were paid modest stipends to work in the Federal Writers Project, the Federal Theatre Project, the Federal Art Project. Their creativity, in the form of novels, murals, plays, performances, public monuments, the providing of music and theater to new audiences, seeded the art and the consciousness of succeeding decades. By 1939 this funding was discontinued.

Federal funding for the arts, like the philanthropy of private arts patrons, can be given and taken away. In the long run art needs to grow organically out of a social compost nourishing to everyone, a literate citizenry, a free, universal, public education complex with art as an integral element, a society honoring both human individuality and the search for a decent, sustainable common life. In such conditions, art would still be a voice of hunger, desire, discontent, passion, reminding us that the democratic project is never-ending.

For that to happen, what else would have to change?

1997

Defying the Space
That Separates

This is a version, slightly revised for the Nation, *of my introduction to the anthology I edited,* Best American Poetry 1996.

I never expected to edit a contemporary poetry anthology. When David Lehman, the series editor for *Best American Poetry,* asked me to undertake a volume, I was dubious—about the title and its implications, about the "catchment area" I could possibly hope to survey, about the usefulness of the project, not only for me but for poetry itself. Who would read it, how would it serve? My decision finally rested on Lehman's guarantee of complete editorial independence, which he honored throughout the selection process.

And so *The Best American Poetry 1996* belies its title. From the first I pushed aside the designations "best" and "American" (surely in the many Americas there are many poetries). Rather, I visualized a gathering of poems that one editor, reading through mailboxes full of journals that publish poetry, found especially urgent, lively, haunting, resonant, demanding to be reread. By temperament, experience and lifework I've been drawn over the past six decades to many kinds of poetry, not always comparable to one another; toward certain kinds of claims for poetry. These inclinations are without doubt reflected in my choices.

But also reflected in this collection—both by what's here and by what is not—are the circumstances of North America (reaching into Mexico) in a decade that began with the Gulf War and that has witnessed accelerated social disintegration, the lived effects of an economic system out of control and antihuman at its core. Contempt for language, the evisceration of meaning from words, are cultural signs that should not surprise us. Material profit finally has no use for other values, in fact reaps benefits from social incoherence and atomization, and from the erosion of human bonds of trust—in language or anything else. And so rapid has been the coming-apart during the years of the nineties in which these poems were being written, so violent the dismantling (of laws, protections, opportunities, due process, mere civilities) that some forget how the history of this Republic has always been a double history, of *selective* and unequal arrangements regarding property, human bodies, opportunity, due process, freedom of expression, civility and much else. What is new: the official abandonment of the *idea* that democracy should be continually expanding, not contracting—an idea that made life more livable for some, more hopeful for others, caused still others to rise to their fullest stature.

"Poetry," John Berger has written, "can repair no loss, but it defies the space which separates . . . by its continual labour of reassembling what has been scattered." As I read throughout the year, I found myself asking, What does it mean for poets when so powerful an idea, prescription, vision of the future—however unrealized—is abruptly abandoned or driven underground? Increasingly it seemed to me that it's not any single poem, or kind of poem, but the coming together of many poems, that can "reassemble what has been scattered," can offer, in Muriel Rukeyser's words, "the truths of outrage and the truths of possibility."

In selecting the poems, I read through a great many literary and cultural journals, requested many others. Early on I sensed that the poetry I was searching for would not be confined to the well-known journals. But I read them in a spirit of hope and discovery, and was sometimes well rewarded. I also sought out many local and regional publications, as well as nonliterary periodicals that publish poems occasionally.

Let me say here what, overall, I was looking for.

I was listening, in all those pages and orderings of words, for music, for pulse and breath, for nongeneric voices.

I was looking for poems with a core (as in *corazón*). The core of a poem isn't something you extract from the poem's body and examine elsewhere; its living energies are manifest throughout, in rhythm, in language, in the arrangement of lines on the page and how this scoring translates into sound. A great many poems rang hollow and monotonous to me; at best they seemed ingenious literary devices, at worst "publish or perish" items for a vita or an M.F.A. dissertation—academic commodities.

I was looking for poetry that could rouse me from fatigue, stir me from grief, poetry that was redemptive in the sense of offering a kind of deliverance or rescue of the imagination, and poetry that awoke delight—lip-to-lip, spark-to-spark, pleasure in recognition, pleasure in strangeness.

I wanted poems from 1995 that were more durable and daring than ever—not drawn from the headlines but able to resist the headlines and the shattering of morale behind them. I was looking for poems that could participate in this historical emergency, had that kind of tensility and beauty. I wasn't looking for up-to-the-minute "socially conscious" verse; I was interested in any poet's acknowledgment of the social and political loomings of this time-space—that history goes on and we are in it. How any poet might take that to heart I could not, would not, attempt to predict. (I also wanted poems good enough to eat, to crunch between the teeth, to feel their juices bursting under the tongue, unmicrowavable poems.)

I was constantly struck by how many poems published in magazines today are personal to the point of suffocation. The columnar, anecdotal, domestic poem, often with a three-stress line, can be narrow in more than a formal sense.

I found—no surprise—that the great majority of poets published in literary magazines are white, yet relationships of race and power exist in their poems most often as silence or muffled subtext if not as cliché. Given the extreme racialization of our social and imaginative life, it's a peculiar kind of alienation that presumes race and racism (always linked to power) will haunt poets of "color" only. Like riches and poverty, like anti-Semitism, whiteness and color have a mythic life that infiltrates poetic language even when unnamed—a legacy of poetic images drawn on racial fantasies, "frozen metaphors," as the critic Aldon Nielsen calls them. The assumptions behind "white" identity in a violently racialized society have their repercussions on poetry, on metaphor, on the civil life in which, for better or worse, oppositionally or imitatively, all art is rooted. For this racialization is more than a set of mythic ideas; it is a system of social and demographic power relations and racially inflected economic policies, and the de factor apartheid of our institutionalized literary culture reflects that system.

Most literary magazines in the United States and Canada are edited by white men (some by white women). A few of these editors clearly try to seek out and publish work that embodies the larger reaches of North American writing and experience. But they do so within a constricting foreground of "raceless" white identity, and usually in "special issues," not as regular practice. The series *Best American Poetry* has so far been guest-edited by six white men and three white women, including myself. The major awards and support grants for poets (such as the Ruth Lilly Poetry Prize, the Kingsley Tufts Award, the Academy of American Poets Fellowship, the Pulitzer Prize and the National Book Critics Circle Award) are administered largely by white judges and bestowed largely on white men. Beyond the recognition involved, which can lead to other opportunities, such prizes do literally allow someone to write— they are inestimable gifts of time. Memberships in the American Academy of Arts and Letters, the American Academy of Arts and Sciences, the Chancellorships of the Academy of American Poets, all vested with the power to distribute other honors, are overwhelmingly passed on by white men to white men, in retention of collegial associations and influence. White women writers are affected by these conditions in that they may be passed over or disregarded as women; but as white people some of us benefit, in a career sense, from this literary apartheid. (James Ledbetter, in *The Village Voice,* and Katha Pollitt, in *The Nation,* have observed the same phenomenon in book and magazine publishing.)

In a more crucial, hands-on sense, no one's work benefits from an artistic climate of restrictive covenants and gated suburbs.

Need I add that when in 1993 an African-American woman delivered her verse at a presidential inauguration, and another African-American woman was named Poet Laureate of the United States, these events did not vitiate the state's racist policies or the general human desolation the state is willing to countenance?

But how could they? What can, and does, open out the field, forward the action for many beleaguered poets and poetries, are projects bringing both literacy and poetry into local workplaces, libraries, reservations and prisons—Laverne Zabielski's The Working Class Kitchen in Lexington, Kentucky; June Jordan's Poetry for the People in the San Francisco Bay Area; the Guild Complex in Chicago; Native Women in the Arts in Toronto; inmate workshops run by groups like the Pelican Bay Information Project in California; and organizations like the National Writers' Voice Project, working through Y.M.C.A.s around the country.

Apartheid of the imagination becomes a blockage in the throat of poetry. It is an artistic problem, a fault line in the tradition; it derives from a devastating social reality, and it cannot be addressed as an artistic problem only. We may feel bitterly how little our poems can do in the face of seemingly out-of-control technological power and seemingly limitless corporate greed, yet it has always been true that poetry can break isolation, show us to ourselves when we are outlawed or made invisible, remind us of beauty where no beauty seems possible, remind us of kinship where all is represented as separation. Poetry, as Audre Lorde wrote long ago, is no luxury. But for our poetry—the poetries of *all* of us—to become equal to a time when so much has to be witnessed, recuperated, revalued, we as poets, we as readers, we as social beings, have large questions to ask ourselves and one another.

Career-minded poets, expending thought and energy on

producing a "publishable manuscript," on marketing their wares and their reputations, as young poets are now urged (and even trained) to do, may have little time left over for thinking about the art itself, ancient and contemporary, and *why* it matters—the state of the art itself as distinct from their own poems and vitas. This shallowness of perspective shows up in reams of self-absorbed, complacent poems appearing in literary magazines, poems that begin, "In the sepia wash of the old photograph . . ."; poems containing far too many words (-computer-driven? anyway, verbally incontinent); poems without music; poems without dissonance; brittle poems of eternal boyishness; poems oozing male or female self-hatred; poems that belabor a pattern until it becomes numbing; poems with epigraphs that unfortunately say it all; poems that depend on brand names; others that depend on literary name-dropping ("I have often thought of Rilke here . . .").

Of course, such templates are not molded solely by a culture of de facto apartheid and a ruthless "market" economy; their use, surely, has to do with individual self-indulgence, passionlessness and passivity. But they have in common the stamp of deep alienation—and obliviousness of that fact. ("Readers of this issue," says the editorial in *The Paris Review*, 134, "may . . . note that a theme seems to run throughout much of the content—namely one of self-destruction. This is, in fact, a coincidence.")

I was also looking for poems that didn't simply reproduce familiar versions of "difference" and "identity." I agree with Charles Bernstein, poet-critic and exponent of L*A*N*G*U*A*G*E poetry, when he remarks in *A Poetics* that "difference" too often appears in poems simply as "subject matter and . . . local color" rather than as "form and content understood as an interlocking figure—the one inaudible without the other." Indeed, there are legions of columnar poems in which the anecdote of an ethnic parent or grandparent is rehearsed in a generic voice and format, whatever the cultural setting. I was glad to find poems by Carolyn Lei-Lanilau, Kimiko Hahn, C. S. Giscombe and Wanda Coleman, among others, that embody dialectics of "otherness" in language itself, the strange and familiar interpenetrating.

But formal innovation alone is not what I was looking for. The most self-consciously innovative, linguistically nonlinear poetry, whatever its theory, can end up as stultifying and as disintegrative as the products of commercial mass media. To hold up the mirror of language to a society in fracture, porous with lying and shrill with contempt for meaning, is not the same thing as creating—if only in the poem itself—another kind of space where other human and verbal relationships are possible. What Toni Morrison calls the "struggle to interpret and perform within a common language shareable imaginative worlds" surely requires keeping that language "endlessly flexible." It also requires vigilance against self-reference and solipsism.

I believe that poems are made of words and the breathing between them: That *is* the medium. I believe as well that poetry isn't language in the abstract but language as in *I want to learn your language. You need more than one language to get by in this city. To learn a language is to earn a soul. She is teaching English as a second language. It is forbidden to use that language in this workplace. A dead language is one that is no longer spoken; it can only be read.*

We need poetry as living language, the core of every language, something that is still spoken, aloud or in the mind, muttered in secret, subversive, reaching around corners, crumpled into a pocket, performed to a community, read aloud to the dying, recited by heart, scratched or sprayed on a wall. *That* kind of language.

Formal innovation always challenges us to "keep the language flexible." It may—or it may not—collaborate (against its own theories) with the rhetoric of deception that seeks to rob language of meaning. I go on searching for poetic means that may help us meet the present crisis of evacuation of meaning.

In the America where I'm writing now, suffering is diagnosed relentlessly as personal, individual, maybe familial, and at most to be "shared" with a group specific to the suffering, in the hope of "recovery." We lack a vocabulary for thinking about pain as communal and public, or as deriving from "skewed social relations" (Charles Bernstein). Intimate revelations may be a kind of literary credit card today, but they don't help us out of emotional overdraft; they mostly recycle the same emotions over and over.

Maturity in poetry, as in ordinary life, surely means taking our places in history, in accountability, in a web of responsibilities met or failed, of received and changing forms, arguments with community or tradition, a long dialogue between art and justice. It means finding our rightful, necessary voices in a greater conversation, its tones, gestures, riffs and rifts. The poems I chose, different from each other in so many ways, ride on stubborn belief in continuity and beauty, in poetry's incalculable power to help us go on.

1996

Poetry and the Public Sphere

At Rutgers University's 1997 conference on "Poetry and the Public Sphere," I was invited to read my work and to make some remarks at a panel on "Poetry, Feminism(s) and the Difficult Wor(l)d." Other panelists were Meena Alexander, Rachel Blau DuPlessis, Susan Stanford Friedman, Alicia Ostriker, and Bob Perelman.

I am enormously pleased to participate in this realization of the visions and work of so many hands, along with poets and readers from so many poetic communities. Recently, I read an essay by Charles Bernstein criticizing a facile multiculturalism that can "have the effect of transforming unresolved ideological divisions and antagonisms into packaged tours of . . . local color of gender, race, sexuality, ethnicity, region, class. . . . In this context, diversity can be a way of restoring a highly idealized conception of a unified American culture that effectively quiets dissent." Many of us, I think, have had our doubts about such a "multiculturalism" or "diversity," or symbolic "inclusion," when the real question in our radically unequal society is power and privilege.

On the other hand, as I read and travel my way around the United States, it's clear that dissenting poetic communities of many kinds are flourishing far from curricular packaging, text-books, and anthologies. When I speak of communities I do not mean poets who speak as one, or readers or listeners for whom a poem works in only one way. Women poets, immigrant poets, prison poets, Latino poets, to name a few, have many voices and many poetic strategies. In this confused and embittered country, poetry is being made and sought at points of stress, at moments of emergence, by unpredictable voices, in unpredictable places. By contrast, a deadly sameness still pervades the poetics of well-known and prestigious literary magazines, and the products of MFA programs, where poems are produced as commodities in the academic marketplace.

I want to give a brief acknowledgment to this panel's title, "Poetry, Feminism(s) and the Difficult Wor(l)d." I take it that poetry—if it is poetry—is liberatory at its core. Not revolution itself, "but a way of knowing / why it must come." I believe there can be no women's liberation under capitalism. Women's liberation—a more concrete and expressive term than "feminism"—will both deliver and be brought to birth by any genuine emancipatory movement. Without women's liberation, no continuing revolution. Without continuing revolution— the long struggle for radical equality—no women's liberation. We cannot hope, or work effectively, for one without the other.

But the thing I want to focus on here is the question of poetry's very medium, language: what we think it can and cannot do, and how. I will draw on two apparently polarized attitudes and try to see what each can offer us. One holds that poetry is pure exploration of language, a kind of "research" into language, which by its rejection of conventional expectations is inherently subversive to dominant and oppressive structures, and to the degradation of language these structures have produced. Poetry that seeks to communicate directly, beyond or beside its formal dynamics, can only fall into collusion with this degradation, this impoverishment, of language. Charles Bernstein, again, has called our public space "befouled" by "spectacularly inequitable distributions of power." In this "befouled" public sphere poetry cannot hope to lend itself to social change through conventional or contaminated methods of communication. Language, the medium, "autonomous and self-sufficient," must do its work by its own methods. I am, of necessity, abbreviating and simplifying here.

In a recent essay in *The Nation,* June Jordan writes of the poetic and activist responses of her Berkeley poetry students to the passage of Proposition 209 in California, the attempt to strike down affirmative action. "They believe someone will come along and listen to what they have to say. . . . They believe that important, truthful conversation between people fosters and defends the values of democratic equality. *They believe that other people deserve supreme efforts of care and honest utterance. . . . They reach for words that create rather than attentuate community"* (emphasis mine). Included in her essay are poems by three of the young poet-activists; they are fresh and passionate political poems.

On the next two pages of *The Nation* are four poems by the winners of the magazine's "Discovery" Prize. Here is the familiar sameness—the well-written, capable mediocrity of American middle-ground status-quo poetry. The poets are neither mining the medium of language for subversive purposes, nor are they reaching for words to create a community of resistance. Subversion is not even an issue here. It struck me, reading them, that the range of "Language" poetics and the range of revolutionary poetics, worldwide, have more in common with each other than either has with this middle ground.

Obviously, I believe language is capable of expressing both simple and complex intentions and meanings, and more—the physicality of our lives. In a country where native-born fascistic tendencies, allied to the practices of the "free" market, have been eviscerating language of meaning, academic postmodern theory has to shoulder its own responsibility for mistrust of the word and attendant paralysis of the will. The public space is indeed befouled. But I also think that Bernstein and others are right when they imply that threadbare language, frozen metaphors, poems in which we "cling to / what we've grasped too well" are part of the problem, and that the power of a poem to subvert, to "intensify / our relationships" depends on its being *poetry*—taking on the medium of language with all its difficulties. Difficulties of relationship and strangeness, of truth-telling and torsion and how the netted bridge is to be suspended over the gorge.

The longer I live, the more history I live through, the more poetries I read and hear aloud, the more I recognize the sheer difficulty and multiplicity of our art, the absolute necessity for it in this time, and the ethical and artistic responsibilities it demands.

I want the tradition of the oral voice in poetry, the remembering of what they tell us to forget. I want the landscape of the visual field on the page, exploding formal verse expectations. I want a poetry that is filmic as a film can be poetic, a poetry that is theater, performance, voice as body and body as voice. I want everything possible for poetry. I want to write, and read, different kinds of poems for different urgencies and kinds of pleasure. I don't believe any single poem can speak to all of us, nor is that necessary; but I believe poems can reach many for whom they were not consciously written, sometimes in ways the poet never expected.

I want to read, and make, poems that are out there on the edge of meaning yet can mean something to the collective. I don't believe it's only the isolated visionary who goes to the edge of meaning; I think the collective needs to go there too, because in fact that edge is where we can see what it would really be like to live without meaning, dissociated.

But I also want to read, and make, poems that remind me "why it must come," why what June Jordan calls the logic of "the infinite connectedness of human life" demands equality in community. This poetry is worth our most sacred and profane passion, because it embodies our desire, what we might create, in the difficult world around the poem.

1997

Muriel Rukeyser:
Her Vision

Written as introduction to the Norton Muriel Rukeyser
Reader, *edited by Jan Heller Levi.*

To enter her work is to enter a life of tremendous scope, the
consciousness of a woman who was a full actor and creator in
her time. But in many ways Muriel Rukeyser was beyond her
time—and seems, at the edge of the twenty-first century, to
have grasped resources we are only now beginning to reach
for: connections between history and the body, memory and
politics, sexuality and public space, poetry and physical science, and much else. She spoke as a poet, first and foremost;
but she spoke also as a thinking activist, biographer, traveler,
explorer of her country's psychic geography.

It's no exaggeration to say that in the work of Muriel
Rukeyser we discover new and powerful perspectives on the
culture of the United States in the twentieth century, "the
first century of world wars," as she called it. Her lifetime
spanned two of them, along with the Spanish Civil War, the
trial of the anarchists Sacco and Vanzetti, the Depression,
the New Deal, the Holocaust, the Cold War and McCarthy

years, the Vietnam War, the renewal of radicalism in the 1960s, the women's liberation movement of the late '60s and '70s, and, throughout, the movements of African-Americans and of working people for survival and dignity. All these informed her life and her art, as did other arts: film, painting, theater, the music of the blues and jazz, of classical orchestras, popular song. From a young age she seems to have understood herself as living in history—not as a static pattern but as a confluence of dynamic currents, always changing yet faithful to sources, a fluid process that is constantly shaping us and that we have the possibility of shaping.

The critic Louise Kertesz, a close reader of Rukeyser and her context, notes that "no woman poet makes the successful fusion of personal and social themes in a modern prosody before Rukeyser." She traces a North American white women's tradition in Lola Ridge, Marya Zaturenska and Genevieve Taggard, all born at the end of the nineteenth century and all struggling to desentimentalize the personal lyric and to write from urban, revolutionary, and working-class experience. In her earliest published poetry, Rukeyser writes herself into the public events unfolding from the year of her birth, and into the public spaces of a great, expansive city. "The city rises in its light. Skeletons of buildings; the orange-peel cranes; highways put through; the race of skyscrapers. And you are part of this."

Rukeyser grew up on Riverside Drive in an upwardly mobile Jewish family—her mother a bookkeeper from Yonkers who counted the poet-scholar-martyr Akiba among her legendary forebears, her father a concrete salesman from Wisconsin who became partner in a sand-and-gravel company. Both loved music and opera, but the house was sparsely supplied with books—"except in the servants' rooms: what do you hear there? *The Man with the Hoe, The Ballad of Reading Gaol.* The little five-cent books . . . read and reread." Rukeyser was sent to Ethical Culture schools and to Vassar, but her father's financial difficulties forced her to leave college. "I was expected to grow up and become a golfer," she recalled—a suburban matron. "There was no idea at that point of a girl growing up to write poems." But she was writing poetry seriously by high school. She was also leading a secret life with the children in her neighborhood, playing in the basements and tunnels beneath the apartment buildings, and noting "the terrible, murderous differences between the ways people lived."

Rukeyser was twenty-one when her *Theory of Flight* received the Yale Younger Poets Prize. Two crucial motifs of her life and work were already unmistakable: the book's title suggests how early she embraced the realm of the technological and scientific imagination; and the opening "Poem out of Childhood" points to her lifelong project of knitting together personal experience with politics. "Knitting together" is the wrong phrase here; in her words, she simply did not allow them to be torn apart.

Any sketch of her life (and here I have space for the merest) suggests the vitality of a woman who was by nature a participant, as well as an inspired observer, and the risk-taking of one who trusted the unexpected, the fortuitous, without relinquishing choice or sense of direction. In 1933, having left Vassar, she went to Alabama and was arrested while reporting on the Scottsboro case. In the years to come she traveled as a journalist to Spain on the eve of the Civil War; to Gauley Bridge, West Virginia, for hearings on a silicon mining disaster; to the opening of the Golden Gate Bridge; to North Vietnam and to South Korea on political journeys. She was disinherited by her family, had a two-months'—long, annulled marriage, bore a son by a different man and raised him in single motherhood. She worked in film and theater, taught at

Vassar, the California Labor School, and Sarah Lawrence College, and was a consultant for the Exploratorium, a museum of science and the arts in San Francisco. A wealthy California woman, out of admiration for her work and recognition of her struggles to earn a living as a single mother, provided an anonymous annual stipend, which Rukeyser gave up after seven years once she held a steady teaching job. She edited a "review of Free Culture" called *Decision,* was hunted as a Communist, was attacked both by conservative New Critics and "proletarian" writers, continued productive as writer and filmmaker, underwent a stroke but survived to write poems about it, and to see her poetry rediscovered by a younger generation of women poets and her *Collected Poems* in print. In 1978 she agreed to speak on a "Lesbians and Literature" panel at the annual convention of the Modern Language Association, but illness precluded her appearing.

Rukeyser's work attracted slashing hostility and scorn (of a kind that suggests just how unsettling her work and her example could be) but also honor and praise. Kenneth Rexroth, patriarch of the San Francisco Renaissance, called her "the best poet of her exact generation." At the other end of the critical spectrum, for the *London Times Literary Supplement* she was "one of America's greatest living poets." She received the Copernicus Prize of the American Academy and Institute of Arts and Letters, and wrote "The Backside of the Academy," celebrating "my street . . . the street I live and write in," its urban vitality and human possibilities unencouraged by the locked doors and formal rituals of the Academy. In her lifetime she was a teacher of many poets, and readers of poetry, and some scientists paid tribute to her vision of science as inseparable from art and history. But she has largely been read and admired in pieces—in part because most readers come to her out of the very separations that her work, in all its phases,

steadfastly resists. We read as feminists, or as literary histori-
ans, or we are searching for a viable Left tradition, and we sift
her pages for our concerns; or we are students of poetry who
assume a scientific biography is irrelevant to us; or we are
trapped in ideas of genre that Rukeyser was untroubled by:
what are passages of poetry doing in a serious political biography? (She called her life of Wendell Willkie "a story and a
song.") Or, meeting her only in anthologies, we meet only the
shorter poems of a great practitioner of the long poem, and
meet her prose not at all. We call her prose "poetic" without
referring to her own definitions of what poetry actually is—an
exchange of energy, a *system of relationships.*

Rukeyser was unclassifiable, thus difficult for canon-makers
and anthologists. She was not a "left wing" poet simply, though
her sympathies more often than not intersected with those of
the organized left, or the various lefts, of her time. Her insis-
tence on the value of the unquantifiable and unverifiable ran
counter to mainstream "scientific attitudes" and to plodding
forms of materialism. She explored and valued myth but came
to recognize that mythologies can rule us unless we pierce
through them, that we need to criticize them in order to move
beyond them. She wrote at the age of thirty-one: "My themes
and the use I have made of them have depended on my life as
a poet, as a woman, as an American, and as a Jew." She saw the
self-impoverishment of assimilation in her family and in the
Jews she grew up among; she also recognized the vulnerabil-
ity and the historical and contemporary "stone agonies" en-
dured by the Jewish people. She remained a secular visionary
with a strongly political sense of her Jewish identity. She wrote
out of a woman's sexual longings, pregnancy, night-feedings, in
a time when it was courageous to do so, especially as she did
it—unapologetically, as a big woman alive in mind and body,
capable of violence and despair as well as desire.

In a very real sense, we learn to read Rukeyser by reading her. She "scatters clews," as she wrote of the charismatic labor organizer Anne Burlak, "clews" that take light from each other, clews that reunite pieces of our experience and thought that we have mistrusted, forgotten, or allowed to be torn from each other. Much that we are taught, much that we live, is of this description. When Rukeyser said that she wrote the biography of the physicist Willard Gibbs because it was a book she needed to read, she could have been speaking of her work as a whole. She wanted to be able to read the life and research of a physicist against the background of the slave trade, of nineteenth-century industrial expansion and urban violence, of the lives of women—intellectuals and factory hands—of Emily Dickinson's poetry and Edison's invention, of Gibbs's own resonances with Melville and Whitman. She wanted to be able to write her own poems in full recognition of the language and imagery of the scientific imagination, the "traces" of the splitting she deplored. Her work was always a process of testing, by the written word and in the most concrete and risk-taking ways, her instincts, making their foundations and meanings visible, first to herself, then to the world.

When Rukeyser is, or appears, "difficult," this may be partly due to resistances stored in us by our own social and emotional training. But it's also true that while she can be direct and linear, she often builds on a nonlogical accumulation of images, glimpses, questions, a process resembling the way our apparently unrelated experiences can build into insight, once connected. This can be an accumulation within a given poem or book of poems, within a prose book, or in the undivided stream of her poetry and her prose. She isn't a writer with a few "gems" that can be extracted from the rest; of all twentieth-century writers, her work repays full reading.

I myself first read Rukeyser in the early 1950s. Like her, I had won the Yale Younger Poets Prize at the age of twenty-one, and I was curious to see what a woman poet, at my age, now ahead of me on the path, had written in her first book. I remember the extraordinary force of the first poem in *Theory of Flight*, how it broke over me, and my envy of the sweeping lines, the authority in that poem. But I was not yet ready to learn from her. *The Life of Poetry* had been published in 1949, the year I began to take myself seriously as a poet, or at least as an apprentice to poetry. No one in the literary world of Cambridge, Massachusetts, where I was a student, spoke of that book as an important resource; young poets were reading Empson's *Seven Types of Ambiguity*, Eliot's *Tradition and the Individual Talent*, I. A. Richards's *Practical Criticism*. Of my professors, only the brilliant and volatile F. O. Matthiessen spoke of Rukeyser, but the poets he taught in his seminar were Eliot, Pound, Williams, Stevens, Marianne Moore, E. E. Cummings. I came to Rukeyser in my maturity, as my own life opened out and I began to trust the directions of my own work. Gradually I found her to be the poet I most needed in the struggle to make my poems and live my life. In the past quarter century, as many silenced voices—especially women's voices—began to bear witness, the prescience and breadth of her vision came clearer to me—for it is a peculiarly relevant vision for our lives on this continent now.

In the 1960s and early '70s Rukeyser and I, together with other poets, often found ourselves on the same platform at readings for groups like RESIST and the Angry Arts Against the War in Vietnam. I never came to know her well; New York has a way of sweeping even the like-spirited into different scenes. But there was an undeniable sense of female power that came onto any platform along with Muriel Rukeyser. She carried her large body and strongly molded head with enormous pride, and stood with presence behind her words. Her poems ranged from political witness to the erotic to the mordantly witty to the visionary. Even struggling back from a stroke, she appeared inexhaustible.

She was, in the originality of her nature and achievement, as much an American classic as Melville, Whitman, Dickinson, Du Bois, or Hurston. It's to be hoped that more of her books will soon be back in print, and still-unpublished writings collected for the first time.

1993

Some Questions
from the Profession

*In December 1998 the Poetry Division of the Modern
Language Association initiated a series of public conversations
between a poet and a group of academic scholar-critics. I was
invited as the first poet in this series. The committee consisted
of Charles Altieri, professor of English at Berkeley; Susan
Stewart, professor of English at the University of Pennsylvania;
Sandra Berman, professor of comparative literature at
Princeton; Peter Quartermain, professor of English at the
University of British Columbia in Vancouver; and Charles
Bernstein, professor of English, the State University of New
York at Buffalo. (Bernstein did not participate in the
interview.)*

*I asked the committee members to provide me in advance
with some of the questions they would be asking. In preparing
for the event, I made notes in response. In fact, not all
questions were asked, and the floor was opened to the
audience. But I found the questions thoroughly interesting, and
have here amplified my responses.*

Charles Altieri: *What is your current thinking on the role of
gender differences in the production and appreciation of poetry? How important for you is gender difference in the framing*

of audience and in the staging of selves within poetry? And what if anything makes poetry written with intense gender positioning available to those not envisioned as its primary audience? How does awareness of those secondary audiences affect you as a poet?

AR: I wonder how often that question is asked of male poets. I began seriously writing in a period (the 1950s to late 1960s) in American poetry that assumed extreme gender positioning—"the poet is a man speaking to men," as Wordsworth had put it even as he was trying to democratize English poetry. And I went through a difficult and isolated process of configuring myself as a poet who was also in a woman's body—writing *Snapshots of a Daughter-in-Law* and many short lyrics in that book, with no encouragement to speak of from the Zeitgeist. It seems obvious to say it now, but poetic materials, images, specific to a female life were implicitly, if not explicitly, devalued and patronized. And the evaluator, the patron, was male.

By the mid-1970s, as a direct offshoot of the women's liberation movement, there were journals and readings and courses emerging all over the country that focused on women's writing—present and past. It seems to me no wonder that Judy Grahn, Audre Lorde, Toi Derricotte, Diane Di Prima, and other poets emerging in this decade were first published by women-owned presses and in radical women's poetry magazines and anthologies. There was a strong sense of having broken not just a male-patrolled barrier, but a racist and heterosexist barrier as well. I can say that with *The Dream of a Common Language* I felt released to write from my whole erotic self, my whole engaged self, though in *The Will to Change* I had been writing more and more explicitly as a woman.

When some men said they felt excluded from this poetry, I

was shocked. We hadn't realized what a huge paradigm shift we were demanding. It wasn't only about women's poetry, it was about the whole construction of male/female relationships, and this could be terrifying to men and to many women.

I had spent years reading black writers and feeling sometimes defensive or unnerved, but never precisely excluded. I understood that blackness and whiteness were intricately involved; that I needed black writing. I wanted to be read by any conceivable reader, but I could hardly return to the kind of poems I had written before 1968. I was profoundly involved with the debates and contradictions of the women's movement, and through it my work was finding a kind of resonance it hadn't had before.

Later, more and more, I heard from men who felt they needed what women were writing, whose first reaction was not defensive and resistant. Many were gay and/or political, many were themselves in revolt against the traditional construction of gender.

But finally the question is: What makes poetry with *any* intense positioning—gender, race, national rootedness, geography—available to those who are not located there?

I think the art of translation has something to teach us about this.

CA: *In your essay on why you refused the National Medal for the Arts, you said that you wanted artists "to work out our connectedness, as artists, with other people who are beleaguered, suffering, disenfranchised, precariously employed workers." How would you respond to those who say that poets, by their education and access to the powers of literacy as well as, at the top, to academic prestige, really cannot share materially in the conditions of the truly disenfranchised, and that claiming such affinities dishonors both poets and those with whom they try to sympathize?*

AR: I'm not sure who the "those" are who say this, but I suspect they feel comfortable in the world as it is, and don't wish to know what makes their lives so comfortable. That desire not to know has persistently impaired intellectual life.

Beyond that I would say, first, that the question artificially and disingenuously tries to conflate art with economic power and academic prestige and so denies the existence of poets and artists from disenfranchised groups. Most artists in this country are "precariously employed."

Second, there are two kinds of forces that bridge huge spaces of difference. One is solidarity, the recognition that we need to join with others unlike ourselves to undo conditions and policies we find mutually intolerable, perhaps for different reasons. This is something more powerful and equalizing than sympathy. The other force is the involuntary emotional connection felt with other human beings, in some unforeseen moment, that can move us out from old automatic affiliations and loyalties into a new and difficult comradeship.

CA: *When I hear you read, I think there are two separate registers of rhythm—one in the syntax as it unfolds and another, more abstract, dimly heard music of large patterns. Are you at all conscious of seeking such effects, and, if you are, can you tell us some of what you do to achieve them, or at least let them come through and not muffle them?*

AR: I'm grateful for this question because it is about music. I am very much aware both of the musical or vocal phrase and of the larger pattern, especially in longer poems. I've been profoundly influenced by music—especially European classical and jazz. I've never analyzed musical patterns, but how could you be listening for years to those great frameworks and not absorb lessons from them? that the micro must work on its own terms within the macro, etc.? Both Bach's passionate contrapuntal sound and the complex sounds of jazz have been my great longtime mentors as to music.

Sandra Berman: *At the end of your poem on René Char in* Midnight Salvage, *a poem I like very much, you speak of "keeping vigil" for this poet. Can you tell me what that means in terms of your own writing, especially your most recent work?*

AR: In that poem "keeping vigil" for René Char means writing the poem. The poem is the vigil. Sometimes one wants to hold up a lighted wick before a certain name. In the case of Char it has to do with the fusion of poetry and active resistance to facism, in his life, with no loss to the poetry. *Leaves of Hypnos* is also a record of an unusual masculinity caught up in war but not deluded by it.

SB: *Your recent book, but also your early poems, clearly engage poetic voices beyond the Anglo-American tradition. Could you tell us which foreign poets have been most important to you over the years? What have they offered to your own poetic itinerary?*

AR: I had studied French in school, with very good teachers, and there were French books in my father's library. I memorized poems by Alfred de Musset and Victor Hugo; went on my own to Baudelaire, Valéry, Apollinaire, much later René Char; Aimé Césaire still later. I read a lot in the original, however badly, always sounding out aloud. Also I read Racine, those great crashing alexandrines. After World War II, there was among my generation a great reaching-out to European poetries—Rilke, Brecht, Montale, Ungaretti, Ekelöf, Nelly Sachs, much later Paul Celan. It was a time when poets in the United States felt a strong interest in and desire for other poetries. The Russians: Akhmatova, Tsvetayeva, Mandelstam, and of course Yevtushenko's and Voznezhensky's onstage performances. I also read Spanish and Latin American poetry—Lorca, Neruda, not always in the best translations—much later, Rosario Castellanos, more recently, Juan Gelman, Vallejo in Clayton Eshleman's great versions.

Living in Holland in the early 1960s, I studied the language, bought an anthology of contemporary Dutch poetry, and, with a dictionary, set about translating poems by Hendrik de Vries, Gerrit Achterberg, Jan Emmens, Leo Vroman. It was my best way to get into the Dutch poetic mind. Then I met the poet and playwright Judith Herzberg and, through her, some of the poets I had been translating. One poet, Chr. J. van Geel, particularly fascinated me and I later used phrases from a poem of his in a poem of my own: "Sleepwalking Next to Death." He was by far the most experimental of the poets I read, and was also a painter.

In New York, I would get involved with a translation project—in the 1960s they were many—such as *A Treasury of Yiddish Poetry*. Irving Howe and Eliezer Greenberg were the editors and asked me to create versions of poems by Kadya Molodowsky, Rachel Korn, and Celia Dropkin. I could use the Dutch I knew in fathoming transliterated versions of Yiddish. Molodowsky's great poem "White Night" made a deep impression on me.

In 1968 I was invited by the Asia Society to be one of a group of American poets participating in a project to translate the seventeenth-century Urdu poet Mirza Ghalib. We were supplied with recordings of the original poems in the ghazal form, historical, cultural, and lexical notes, and literal translations, by the editor, Aijaz Ahmad. For me, this project led to new poetic strategies, including a long poem, distinctly American, in modified ghazal form.

Without translations from other languages I would have been severely deprived—unaware of the poetry of Yannis Rit-

sos, Nazim Hikmet, Mahmoud Darwish, to name a few—not
to speak of Sappho and Dante.

I can't emphasize enough how much my poetry has been
stretched, enlarged, strengthened, fortified, by the non-Anglo-
American poetries I have read, tangled with, tried to hear and
speak in their original syllables, over the years.

Susan Stewart: *In your most recent book,* Midnight Salvage,
*you end by speaking of the "ever changing" nature of human
language. Do you see the practice of lyric as a chance to inter-
vene in language's changes—in other words, is changing the
language a means to changing consciousness?*

AR: If by "the practice of lyric" you mean the whole process
of writing poetry, I feel the relation of consciousness and language is dialectical. In making poetry, or any kind of art, we're
translating into a medium—in this case language—the contents of our consciousness, wherever they may come from, let
alone the huge underground beneath consciousness. And then
poetry becomes something that can enter the consciousness of
others—primarily and centrally through language, but language "charged with meaning to the uttermost"—through images, aural reverberations, the texture of verbal relationships
within a poem, the actual image a poem makes on the page,
the different voices within the poem, the playing-off of all this
on the reader's underground life. A poem, then, could be one
influence on consciousness—I would hope, in the direction of
enlarging the imagination and not shrinking it. I don't believe
that there is only one way to do this. Many kinds of poetry act
on our consciousness in many different ways, and at different
times in our lives.

Peter Quartermain: *Do you really want "a common language"?*

AR: The phrase "the dream of a common language" is the title of a book I wrote in the early 1970s, and it comes from a poem in that book, "Origins and History of Consciousness," in which I say, "No one lives in this room / without confronting the whiteness of the wall / behind the poems, planks of books / photographs of dead heroines. / Without contemplating last and late / the true nature of poetry. The drive / to connect. The dream of a common language."

Now that phrase, like the title of that book, has sometimes been read, or heard, as, variously, a call for a literal world language, like Esperanto!, or for a "women's language," or something like what French feminist theorists called "écriture féminine." But what I had in mind was poetry itself as connective urge and power. Do I want that? Yes. Do I want it in a literal sense, that each word or line I write has the same meaning for everyone as it does for me? No. Do I think poems are made of words used according to dictionary definitions? Obviously not. But poetry is an art of translation, a connective strand between unlike individuals, times, and cultures.

PQ: *In the last twenty-five years, quite a few women (e.g., Beverly Dahlen, Rachel Blau DuPlessis, Kathleen Fraser, Judy Grahn, Susan Howe, Maureen Owen, Joan Retallack) have explored gender identity through so-called "experimental" writing. How do you see your own work in relation to theirs?*

AR: In the early 1980s, Kathleen Fraser and Rachel Blau Du-Plessis kindly had their journal *(HOW)ever* sent to me, and I read it with interest. My own concerns at that time were different. I was involved in a part of the United States women's movement that was grappling with differences among women—race and class being at the fore—more than with art and gender identity. Grahn's *A Woman Is Talking to Death* affected me profoundly, and I later wrote a foreword to her collected poems, *The Work of a Common Woman*.

It wasn't that I was indifferent to "innovative" writing—I was searching for new strategies from the early 1960s on, as in *Snapshots of a Daughter-in-Law*; I think it's obvious in poems like "Shooting Script," "The Burning of Paper Instead of Children," "Ghazals: Homage to Ghalib," and "Leaflets." But most of the work in *(HOW)ever* seemed a bit aside from the questions that were haunting me then.

One of the things that has fascinated me is, How do you make poetry out of political experiences—not *about*, but *out of*, the questions and passions that drive a collective movement? a political life? That's the kind of thing I was trying to do in "Yom Kippur 1984," or, later, in parts of "Inscriptions," and more recently in "A Long Conversation." I want to add that the work of many of the women poets you mention has provoked me, in the best sense, to look at my own work critically.

PQ: *Creeley, Duncan, Ginsberg, Olson—male writers who, perhaps, in the 1960s tried to take American poetry on courses quite different from your own: you looked in another direction. What do you think of them now?*

AR: In the early 1960s Denise Levertov introduced me to the work of Creeley, Duncan, and Olson. Also, of course, Williams, though I'd read him a bit before. But my own life, also, was pushing me into kinds of poetry I hadn't written before. Over the years, I was to draw in my own way on their (very different) poetics, but more on the poetry itself. The title and epigraph of *The Will to Change* are from Olson's "The Kingfishers." Duncan's "A Poem Beginning with a Line by Pindar" showed me that you can bring together in one poem the contemporary with the visionary. It probably affected my writing of the poem "Leaflets" just that that poem was there. Ginsberg I wasn't drawn to, though "Howl" and "Kaddish" at their moment did seem strikingly and outrageously new. But I've gone back more and more to Creeley, Duncan, and Olson in recent years. More recently to George Oppen, Robin Blaser.

Influence is a multifarious thing. You might be resisting a certain poetry intellectually and emotionally while absorbing it at some more intuitive level, taking what you can use. I'm fairly omnivorous. Poetries of many kinds and periods have taught me things I needed—so have films, histories, political philosophies, song lyrics, visual art, pamphlets, etc.

A poet's problems—the materials she has to grapple with— are infinitely expanding and require a multiplicity of approaches. A lot of poets in the United States today box themselves in too easily—what my old friend Hugh Seidman once called "a poetry of false problems." I think what he meant was that conventional problems are given conventional solutions, already arrived at. Even an "experimental" solution can be conventional if it merely repeats an old experiment, doesn't recognize it has to struggle with a different problem—or with an old problem in a different way. A male poet who is frozen into conventional male entitlements can only be conventional however "experimental" his use of language. A white poet who is frozen into metaphors of race, likewise. People think it's just about "politics," but it's equally a question of art.

In poetry you need everything you can get your hands on, so you look back and forward and sideways. You are, in a word, avid.

1998

Interview with Rachel Spence

These questions and answers were faxed back and forth between London and California in the course of an interview for the Jewish Quarterly: A Magazine of Contemporary Writing and Culture. *The interview, in a different form, was published in autumn 1999.*

Rachel Spence: *In your most recent work, you are writing from, in your own words, "a theatre of voices." Why have you chosen to work with and from these fragmented identities?*

AR: I don't think of the voices in my recent work as "fragmented identities" any more than I see the characters in a play or a novel as "fragmented identities." Today, there's a banalizing tendency to read all literature as autobiographical, to discount the real work of the imagination. I've been creating characters as the novelist or playwright might. The literature of the restricted "I" becomes too limiting after a while, too claustrophobic.

I have always been interested in characters and situations that are not my own, going back to very early work—my first book in fact. More recently I've listened to voices, imagined narratives, the white girl runaway in "Harpers Ferry," (in *Time's Power*) "Marghanita" and the characters in the opening section of the title poem in *An Atlas of the Difficult World,* the various speakers in "Inscriptions" or "Six Narratives" in *Dark Fields of the Republic,* and, of course, the voices in "A Long Conversation" in *Midnight Salvage.* I also include the presence or actual words of historical figures, including but not limited to writers. I think if you go back to *Snapshots of a Daughter-in-Law,* from the early 1960s, you will find such voices. So this is not a new occurrence in my work.

But I want to say again that poetry is work done from the imagination, in the medium of language, and I deplore the diminishment of that possibility, when poems are treated as personal biography or as paraphrasable narratives.

RS: *Increasingly your poetry presents a vehement critique of capitalist North America, whilst paying tribute to individuals who have resisted, and finding value in private intimacies and natural beauty. Although your identity as a feminist and lesbian emerges seamlessly through the writing, gender and sexuality no longer take centre stage in the majority of your poems. How has this evolution come about?*

AR: Gender and sexuality have been crucial to my work from the beginning: there are poems in my first book, published when I was twenty-one, that (more or less encodedly) wrestle with those questions. I first took them up head-on in *Snapshots of a Daughter-in-Law* when writing about such things from a critical or nontraditional perspective was pretty taboo. By the mid-1960s, there were political movements in the United States that were challenging the way things were, challenging many kinds of authority, and these cleared space for a women's movement that made gender and sexuality central issues.

For a while, encouraged and sustained by a vigorous

women's print and arts movement (presses, newspapers, film collectives, literary/political journals), it was possible for the first time to explore these questions in poetry and prose, and feel resonance from other artists making similar explorations in painting, theater, film. That's a tremendously liberating and nourishing condition in which to work.

With Reagan's election in 1980 many things changed. Antifeminism was central to the right-wing "family" strategy, but so was the defamation of every past social justice movement. I recall in England Thatcher's dictum "There Is No Alternative." Here, too, particularly given our national history of anticommunism and anti-socialism, the possibility of an alternative has been rubbed out and discredited.

It's not that I set out, in the 1980s, to write poetry that would "address" these conditions. Rather, I felt my inner and outer life threatened by the politics of arrogance and cruelty, and that sense of danger and disturbance began to enter my poetry. I thought often about the Weimar period in Germany, which led to the election of Hitler; "Then or Now," the sequence in *Dark Fields of the Republic,* came out of that, trying to imagine the way fascism can work on consciousness—not trying to equate this time with 1930s Germany, but to use history as a way of looking at our own time and place, our own self-deceptions, our desire not to know what is going on.

What drives my poetry, always, is the need to see revealed what isn't necessarily apparent or obvious—to uncover "lies, secrets, and silences." For me it is always a question of language as a probe into the unknown or unfamiliar. In the 1950s and early 1960s gender and sexuality were a field of lies, secrets, and silences. I didn't make poetry out of theories; I wrote from the need to make open and visible what was obscure and unspeakable.

It always surprises me when people write of my work as if I

had taken up the cudgels for the "underprivileged" or the "oppressed," as a kind of missionary work. I write from absolute inner necessity, responding to my location in time and place, trying to find a language equal to that.

RS: *In* Midnight Salvage, *you constantly allude to and quote historical figures of resistance. Why are you drawn now more than ever to the art and voices of the revolutionary?*

AR: I think I've brought figures of resistance into my poetry for quite a while—going back to the voice of Mary Wollstonecraft in "Snapshots of a Daughter-in-Law" (1960). History has always felt to me an immense resource for art, and poetry as a place where history can be kept alive—not grand master narratives, but otherwise forgotten or erased people and actions. In the 1970s we were rediscovering women whose lives had been dropped out of history or distorted, like Susan B. Anthony, Harriet Tubman, Emily Dickinson, Marie Curie, Ida B. Wells-Barnett, Hannah Senesch, Ethel Rosenberg. In *Midnight Salvage* there's the poem drawn from René Char's resistance journals, and the one for Tina Modotti, but also the many characters, both historical and invented, male and female, who I listen in on in "A Long Conversation." I'm not trying to iconize, but to lay an ear to what's under the surface.

RS: *In "An Atlas of the Difficult World" the last stanza speaks to various readers, all of whom are in some way in difficulty. In these lines, you seem acutely aware of your responsibilities as an artist. Has your sense of these responsibilities changed? Has your perception of your audience changed?*

AR: In the last section of "Atlas" I was trying to imagine an invisible collectivity. These are not people in extraordinary difficulty; they are ordinary people trying to live their lives. "Atlas" evokes a United States in fracture, not only in the present but going back to the beginning of European contact. Throughout the poem I'm asking questions of the past, probing the dissonance between our national self-image and the historical reality. The next to last section is a love poem to a woman, and the last section tries to imagine all these lives into which, for a moment, a poem might fall—amid the necessities of everyday life those possible readers are facing.

For me it's less about the responsibilities of the artist than about the need for art in many kinds of lives, a need shared with others we may never know. In *What Is Found There*, I talk about poetry as "a wick of desire" that helps keep alive in us the capacity to resist, to imagine, to change.

RS: *Historically, much of your poetry has emerged out of the different strands of your identity—in your own words, "split at the root." Do you still feel that split as acutely as ever, and if not, can you say what has helped to heal it?*

AR: Back in the early 1960s I wrote the poem ("Readings of History") in which the lines occur: "Split at the root, neither Gentile nor Jew, / Yankee nor Rebel, born / in the face of two ancient cults." But the next line is, "I'm a good reader of histories." That poem is very interesting to me now because it's asking the question, Why does history matter? Why know it? And the poem suggests that the present seems too deranged, too fragmented, too incoherent, unless you have a sense of the past. Now, that is a very Jewish perception, it seems to me.

RS: *Could you elaborate a little?*

AR: I don't mean to imply that Jews have a unique need for, or consciousness about, history—but that for us, history has

been a way of living with the often-chaotic present and holding on to a longer and larger view. Kadya Molodowsky, the
Yiddish poet, writes:

> **Pack up my chaos with its gold-encrusted buttons**
> **Since chaos will always be in fashion . . .**

But about history, its contours are always changing, the way
a landscape changes in snow or fog or sunlight, as new explorations uncover new truths—or untruths. That doesn't inval-
idate it, though.

RS: *What has being Jewish meant to you? And has this meaning changed as you've grown older?*

AR: Being Jewish has meant being a question, not only as in
"the Jewish Question," but as a woman, a lesbian, a patrilin-
eal Jew, a non-Zionist, within the whole argument and con-
testation about "being Jewish." Being Jewish meant that at
sixteen, an American girl in Baltimore, I took the streetcar
downtown and watched the first newsreels of the death camps
and had to store that inside myself for a long time—my parents did not talk about it. For a long time the Holocaust was
almost a taboo subject among American Jews—as among
other Americans. The historical event was pushed under the
rug in the late 1940s and the 1950s. At the same time, in that
period, the McCarthy period, "Jew" was linked with "Communist"—hence un-American.

I'm an American Jew. I could lay claim both to a history of
accommodation and attempted assimilation and a history of
internationalist radicalism. I'm not a Jew from Eritrea, Łódź
Rhodes, Argentina, Montreal, Melbourne, India, Israel,
Britain, Chile, though I know we're all connected.

The way I think we are connected is through a paradigm that Jews have shared with other peoples, including of course Arabs—a paradigm of the pariah, suspect, marginalized, easily scapegoated, dispossessed. Like other such peoples, we also have a culture that has enriched the world.

When Jews turn others into scapegoats, dispossess or dehumanize them, destroy their homes and communities, I have to say, yes, we Jews do this. And I'm passionately opposed to it.

At the same time I feel very connected to organizations like Jews for Racial and Economic Justice in New York City, or Jews Against Genocide, which carry on a consciously Jewish tradition of activism, very much derived from the wave of Jewish immigrants in the early twentieth century who brought along their socialist, secular bundles of vision.

I'm not a religious Jew. I'm a secular person. I have friends who are rabbis, and I admire their learning, their standing up to claim the religion as women and as gay men. But my passions lie with activism and with a desire for greater solidarity among peoples of the paradigm, as you might call us.

Being Jewish took me into specifically Jewish political work in the 1980s. I joined a national organization of progressive Jews, New Jewish Agenda. It lasted about a decade and was a focus for political action for Jewish activists in many areas: racial and economic justice, feminism, Central America solidarity, the Middle East. We were working for a two-state solution in Israel/Palestine long before the Oslo Accords. Most American Jewish organizations saw us as pariahs for taking this position. We were constantly under attack for even suggesting the necessity of a Palestinian state. That organization dispersed—for lack of funds, uncertain leadership, virulent opposition—but many of us who were part of it still keep in touch, and out of it came the Jewish feminist magazine *Bridges,* which I helped cofound.

RS: *In which directions is your work now moving?*

AR: I don't know, if in that question you mean a planned trajectory. I have no such thing. I have thought recently that my poetry exposes the scarring of the human psyche under the conditions of a runaway, racist capitalism. But that's because my psyche is also scarred by these conditions. One of the things that most attracts me to Marx is his sense that exploitative relations of production end by affecting *all* human relationships, the most private and intimate included. It's seemed to me that if I could show that, in art, I would be making a kind of sense for our time.

But at the same time I want never to let go of the other— the humanly possible.

RS: *Could you say more about what that phrase means to you?*

AR: There's a colloquial American expression, "I'll do anything humanly possible," to help you get a job, be at your sickbed, get to that meeting, etc., etc. I'm leaning on that phrase, asking, What *is* humanly possible if we require something beyond the horrible culture of production for profit? Human beings aren't merely determined by capitalist production—Marx never said that. These are conditions "not of our choosing" in which we can make history. What's "humanly possible" might be what we bring to the refusal to let our humanity be stolen from us.

It may seem aggrandizing to say that poetry can have a hand in this, but I believe it can, in its own way and on its own terms.

1999

Arts of the Possible

Given as the Troy Lecture, University of Massachusetts, Amherst, in April 1997. First published in the Massachusetts Review, *autumn 1997.*

I appreciate this opportunity to pull together and present some issues I've been wrestling with over the past couple of years. In fact, I confess that I've kept for more than eighteen months a folder labeled "Troy Lecture" into which I've been sliding handwritten and typewritten notes, made in various states of intense reflection, disquietude, and hope. When I shook this folder out on the kitchen table last January, its contents did not miraculously assemble themselves into the outline of a lecture, as the mountain of peas, beans, and grains sorted themselves out for Psyche in the Greek myth. But they did remind me how persistently certain realities and urgencies had been haunting me over a period of time, ineluctable visitors it seemed.

Psyche's task was to separate legume from groat, millet grain from lentil. I see mine, rather, as a work of connection.

Let me first sketch out some of my concerns, then try to show how I think they inhere with this lectureship's focus on art, the humanities, and public education—and with conditions facing all of us, but especially the young who are trying to make sense of their lives in this time.

I begin with the abrupt reshuffling of our once apparently consensual national project: a democratic republic with a large and growing middle class, and equality of opportunity as its great hope. Over the past two decades or less, we have become a pyramidic society of the omnivorously acquisitive few, an insecure, dwindling middle class, and a multiplying number of ill-served, throwaway citizens and workers—finally, a society accused by the highest incarceration rate in the world. We dangle over an enormous gap between national propaganda and the ways most people are actually living: a cognitive and emotional dissonance, a kind of public breakdown, with symptoms along a spectrum from acute self-involvement to extreme anxiety to individual and group violence.

Along with this crisis in our own country I have been thinking about the self-congratulatory self-promotion of capitalism as a global, transnational order, superseding governments and the very meaning of free elections. I have especially been noting the corruptions of language employed to manage our perceptions of all this. Where democracy becomes "free enterprise," individual rights the self-interest of capital, it's no wonder that the complex of social policies needed to further democratic equality is dismissed as a hulk of obsolete junk known as "big government." In the vocabulary kidnapped from liberatory politics, no word has been so pimped as *freedom*.

I've been struck by the presumption, endlessly issuing from the media, in academic discourse, and from liberal as well as conservative platforms, that the questions raised by Marxism, socialism, and communism must inexorably be identified with their use and abuse by certain repressively authoritarian regimes of the twentieth century: therefore they are henceforth to be nonquestions. That because Marxism, socialism, communism were aliases employed by certain stagnating, cruel, and unscrupulous systems, they have and shall have no other existence than as masks for those systems. That American capitalism is the liberatory force of the future with a transnational mission to quench all efforts to keep these questions alive. That capitalism's violence and amorality are somehow nonaccountable. That communist or socialist parties all over the world, including those of India and South Africa, imitate the degraded communisms of eastern Europe and China.

In this particular presumption, or dogma, capitalism represents itself as a law of history or, rather, a law beyond history, beneath which history now lies, corroding like the *Titanic*. Or, capitalism presents itself as obedience to a law of nature, man's "natural" and overwhelming predisposition toward activity that is competitive, aggressive, and acquisitive. Where capitalism invokes freedom, it means the freedom of capital. Where, in any mainstream public discourse, is this self-referential monologue put to the question?

The monologue may claim to be transnational, but its roots are in Western Europe and the United States, and in the United States we have our own idioms. We're still rehearsing an old, disabling rhetoric, invoking the "free" climate and virgin resources awaiting the first Europeans on this continent, the "free" spirit of individualism and laissez-faire that allowed penniless new arrivals to acquire lands and fortunes. Generally speaking, we don't trace American opportunity, prosperity, and global power to the genocide of millions of Indians, the claiming and contaminating of Indian lands and natural resources, the presently continuing repression of Indian life and leadership; nor to that Atlantic slave trade which underwrote the wealth of Europe by introducing a captive labor force into both Americas and the Caribbean, and brought the "New World" into the international economy.

We may have heard that the era of modern slavery is finished, is "history," that the genocide against tribal peoples and the expropriation of land held in trust by them are over and done with along with the last wagon trains. But such institutions and policies do not die—they mutate—and we are living them still: they are the taproots of the economic order that has taken "democracy" as its alias. Our past is seeded in our present and is trying to become our future.

These concerns engage me as a citizen, feeling daily in my relationships with my fellow citizens the effects of a system based in the accumulation of wealth—the value against which all other values must justify themselves. We all feel these effects, almost namelessly, as we go about our individual lives and as the fragments of a still ill-defined people.

But these are also my concerns as a poet, as the practitioner of an ancient and severely tested art. In a society in such extreme pain, I think these are any writer's, any artist's, concerns: the unnamed harm to human relationships, the blockage of inquiry, the oblique contempt with which we are depicted to ourselves and to others, in prevailing image making; a malnourishment that extends from the body to the imagination itself. Capital vulgarizes and reduces complex relations to a banal iconography. There is hate speech, but there is also a more generally accepted language of contempt and self-contempt—the term *baby boomers,* for instance, infantilizes and demeans an entire generation. In the interests of marketing, distinctions fade and subtleties vanish.

This devaluation of language, this flattening of images, results in a massive inarticulation, even among the educated. Language itself collapses into shallowness. Everything indeed tends toward becoming a *thing* until people can speak only in terms of the *thing,* the inert and always obsolescent commodity. We are, whatever our generation, marked as "consumers"—but what of the human energy we put forth, the actual needs we feel as distinct from the pursuit of consumption? What about the hunger no commodity can satisfy because it is not a hunger for something on a shelf? Or the hunger forced to *consume* the throwaway dinners in a fast-food restaurant dumpster?

Any artist faces the necessity to explore, by whatever means, human relationships—which may or may not be perceived as political. But there are also, and always, the changing questions of the medium itself, the craft and its demands.

The study of silence has long engrossed me. The matrix of a poet's work consists not only of what *is there* to be absorbed and worked on, but also of what is missing, *desaparecido,* rendered unspeakable, thus unthinkable. It is through these invisible holes in reality that poetry makes its way—certainly for women and other marginalized subjects and for disempowered and colonized peoples generally, but ultimately for all who practice any art at its deeper levels. The impulse to create begins—often terribly and fearfully—in a tunnel of silence. Every real poem is the breaking of an existing silence, and the first question we might ask any poem is, *What kind of voice is breaking silence, and what kind of silence is being broken?*

And yet I need to say here that silence is not always or necessarily oppressive, it is not always or necessarily a denial or extinguishing of some reality. It can be fertilizing, it can bathe the imagination, it can, as in great open spaces—I think of those plains stretching far below the Hopi mesas in Arizona—be the nimbus of a way of life, a condition of vision. Such living silences are more and more endangered throughout the world, by commerce and appropriation. Even in conversation, here in North America, we who so eagerly unpack our most private concerns before strangers dread the imaginative space that silence might open between two people or within a group. Television, obviously, abhors such silence.

But the silence I abhor is dead silence, like a dead spot in an auditorium, a dead telephone, silence where language needed to be and was prevented. I am talking about the silence of a Lexan-sealed isolation cell in a maximum security prison, of evidence destroyed, of a language forbidden to be spoken, a vocabulary declared defunct, questions forbidden to be asked. I am also thinking of the dead sound of senseless noise, of verbal displacement, when a rich and active idiom is replaced by banal and inoffensive speech, or words of active courage by the bluster of false transgression, crudely offensive yet finally impotent.

Never has the silence of displacement been so deafening and so omnipresent. Poetic language lives, labors, amid this displacement; and so does political vision.

I've been reflecting—not so much nostalgically as critically—on the early 1970s, when the emergent women's liberation movement was pouring its vitality into a great many channels: organizing, theorizing, institution building, communications, the arts, research, and journalism. For most of the women engaged with that movement, at least for a while, there was an unforgettable sense of coming alive, of newness and connectedness. You could feel the power of a social critique, a politics, that seemed capable of clarifying previously mystified and haunted terrain. Seeded for over a century in the continuity of other movements for justice—labor, anti-lynching, civil rights, anti-imperialism, antimilitarism, socialism—it called those movements to account for perpetuating old injuries of misogyny, old sexual divisions of power.

A certain elasticity of economic opportunities and means in that period, combined with intense intellectual and creative ferment, made it possible to imagine hitherto nonexistent resources and then work to realize them: women's centers for politics and culture, rape-crisis hotlines and counseling, action groups for reproductive rights, safe houses for battered women and their children, feminist health clinics and credit unions, and also feminist and lesbian presses, newspapers, arts journals, bookstores, theater, film and video collectives, cultural workshops and institutes. As always, the new liberatory politics broke open new cultural and intellectual space. For a period at least, political analysis and activism were interactive with cultural work, and "women's culture" had not broken itself off from "women's liberation."

Quite apart from the media's brief blaze of attention on a few white faces, the movement created its own spaces for dissent and disputation. The very idea of a monolithic movement was disputed early on by working-class women, by socialist feminists, by women of color, by lesbians, by women who were all of these. There were confrontations about hierarchy and democracy, about which women speak for women and how and why; about sexuality; about how racial and class separations frame what we see and how we set about organizing. There were the tenacity and courage of those who stood up in meeting after meeting to say again what others did not want to hear: that the basic facts of inequality and power in North America cannot be addressed in gender terms only.

Granting authority to women's experience as that which has been disprized, distorted, obliterated, this movement also had to reckon with the fact that on the other side of silence women have enormous *differences* of experience.

"Identity politics" was one attempt to address this contradiction. I first encountered the term in a much-discussed and widely reprinted black feminist manifesto, the Combahee River Collective statement, first published in 1977. This "identity politics" was a necessary response to the devaluation and invisibility of African American women in all movements, but it was implicitly and explicitly seen as moving toward solidarity. The project of changing structures of inequality would be carried on from a self-conscious and analytic knowledge of one's own location in the intersections of gender, race, class, sexual orientation. This self-consciousness was a necessary step toward the self-definition of African American women against both white and male self-universalizing, but it was not an end in itself. The collective voiced its own "need to do political work and to move beyond consciousness-raising and serving exclusively as an emotional support group."

Had such a reading of "identity politics" been responsively taken up by a critical mass of white women, it might have led us to see—and act on—the racialization of *our* lives, how our experiences of color and class were shaped by capitalist patriarchy's variant and contradictory uses for different female identities. As the 1980s wore on, "identity" became a synonym for "safe space" in which alikeness rather than difference could be explored. An often stifling self-reference and narrow group chauvinism developed.

Meanwhile, capitalism lost no time in rearranging itself around this phenomenon called "feminism," bringing some women closer to centers of power while extruding most others at an accelerating rate. A narrow identity politics could easily be displayed on a buffet table of lifestyles by the caterers of personal solutions. We are learning that only a politics of the whole society can resist such assimilation.

I have focused briefly on the women's liberation movement both because of my own ongoing stake in it and because it embodied for a while the kind of creative space a liberatory political movement can make possible: "a visionary relation to reality." Why this happens has something to do with the sheer power of a collective imagining of change and a sense of collective hope. Coming together with others to define common desires and needs, and to identify the forces that frustrate them, can be a strong tonic for the imagination. And there has been a vital dynamic between art—here I speak particularly of writing, a seizing of language, a transformation of subjectivity—and the continuing life of movements for social transformation. Where language and images help us name and recognize ourselves and our condition, and practical activity for liberation renews and challenges art, there is a complementarity as necessary as the circulation of the blood. Liberatory politics is, after all, not simply opposition but an expression of the impulse to create the new, an expanding sense of what's *humanly possible.*

The movements of the 1960s and the 1970s in the United States were openings out of apertures previously sealed, into collective imagination and hope. They wore their own blinders, made their own misjudgments. They have been relentlessly trivialized, derided, and demonized by the Right and by what's now known as the political center. They have also been disparaged, as Aijaz Ahmad notes, in many of the texts of postmodernism, as mere "false consciousness" or "folly," while in academic critical theory Marxist or socialist thought may be dismissed outright or treated "as a method primarily of *reading.*"

In this time of manic official optimism and much public denial and despair, I know that the present generation of students must and will negotiate their own ways among such claims. Yet when I think of the political education of students now in college, I have to think of the political silences and displacements of the past twenty years. I think of the fabric of discussion, the great rents in that fabric, about the packaging and marketing of each generation's prefabricated desires and needs.

I have deplored the retreat into the personal as a current fetish of mass-market culture. The conglomerate publishing industry stays afloat in part on a blurry slick of heavily promoted self-help literature, personal memoirs by early bloomers, celebrity biographies, the packaging of authors complete with sex scandals and lawsuits. From television talk shows and interviews you might deduce that all human interactions are limited to individual predicaments, family injuries, personal confessions and revelations.

The relationship of the individual to a community, to social power, and to the great upheavals of collective human experience will always be the richest and most complex of questions. The blotted-out question might well be: With any personal history, what is to be done? What do we know when we know your story? *With whom do you believe your lot is cast?*

If I seem to come down hard on "the personal," it's not because I undervalue individual experience, or the human impulse to narrative, or because I believe in any kind of simplistic "universal"—male or female, old or new. Garrett Hongo gives an eloquent account of the personal essay as one means for a community to come to know itself, to reject both external and internal stereotyping, to hear "stories that are somehow forbidden and tagged as aberrational, as militant, as depraved."

For a writer, as you live in this kind of silence, in this kind of misery, not knowing quite what it is that the world is not giving you, . . . that your work cannot address as yet, you are at the beginning of a critique of culture and society. It is the moment when powerful personal alienation slips into critical thinking—the origin of imagination. It is this initial step of intellection that enables the emergence of new, transformative, even revolutionary creativity. It occurs at the juncture between the production of art and the exercise of deep critical thought.

Conglomerate publishing and marketing have little interest in such junctures.

I have been trying to decipher the moral ecology of this nonaccountable economy, this old order calling itself new. What are its effects on our emotional and affectional and intellectual life? Over the past decade I would have found it harder to look steadily and long at the scene around us without using Marx's perception that economic relationships—the relationships of production—will, unchecked, infiltrate all other social relationships at the public and the most private levels. Not that Marx thought that feelings, spirit, human relationships are just inert products of the economy. Rather, he was outraged by capital's treatment of human labor and human energy as a means, its hostility to the development of the whole person, its reduction of the entire web of existence to commodity: what can be produced and sold for profit. *In place of all the physical and spiritual senses,* he tells us, *there is the sense of possession, which is the alienation of all these senses.* Marx was passionate about the insensibility of a system that must extract ever more humanity from the human being: time and space for love, for sleep and dreaming, time to create art, time for both solitude and communal life, time to explore the idea of an expanding universe of freedom.

For a few years now, the Republican Congress and the Right have been repetitiously characterized by the term *mean-spirited.* By extension, the same phrase has been used to describe the mood of the disgruntled American voter. I have always found this term suspiciously off the mark. If it were only a matter of spirits! Mean-spiritedness has been as American as cherry pie—alongside other tendencies: it has designated a parochial or provincial strain in a greater social texture.

Mean-spiritedness as a generalized social symptom suggests an inexplicable national mood, a bad attitude, a souring of social conscience and compassion. But people don't succumb to sourness, resentment, and fear for no reason. The phrase directs us toward social behavior but not to the economic relationships that Marx perceived as staining all social behavior. It refers to attitude but not to policies and powers and the interests they serve. It's a diversionary piece of cant that obscures the lived impact of increasingly cruel legislation and propaganda against poor people, immigrants, women, children, youth, the old, the sick—all who are at risk to begin with—and that also masks the erosion of modest middle-class hopes, in the name of the market or of a chimera known as the balanced budget.

We have all seen attempts to graph numerically the effects of these policies: numbers of people who have slid from apartments or rented rooms or splintered households into the streets; a population of working people without health care, child care, safe and affordable shelter. But each of these people is more than a body to be counted: each is a mind and a soul. Numbers of children left alone or in the care of other children so parents can work; of children doing time in schools that are no more than holding pens for youth and lethal for many. Each of these children possesses an intelligence, creative urge, and capacity that cannot be accounted for by quantifying. Numbers of working people, blue-collar and white-collar, who have lost full-time jobs with pensions to so-called downsizing and restructuring and the export of the production process—working several jobs piecemeal for eversinking wages and with mandatory overtime. Each of these people is more than a pinpoint on a chart: each was born to her or his own usefulness and uniqueness. Numbers of prisons now under construction—a "growth industry" in this country, whose public schools and urban hospitals are disintegrating. These prisons, too, are holding pens for youth, disproportionately so for young African American men. The prison as shadow factory, where inmates assemble, at 35 cents an hour, parts for cars and computers, or take telephone reservations for TWA and Best Western—a captive cheap labor force. Women—of all colors—are the fastest growing incarcerated group, two-thirds being mothers of dependent children. A growing population of lifers and people on death row. A death-penalty system tabulated strenuously to race. In the words of the death-row journalist Mumia Abu-Jamal, "the barest illusion of rehabilitation [is being] replaced by dehumanization by design" in the maximum-security, sensory-deprivation units of the penal system in the United States, and in prison policies overall.

Each of these women and men "inside" has, or once had, a self to offer the world, a presence. And the slippage toward prison of those "outside"—so many of them young—who feel themselves becoming social and economic discards, is a process obscured by catchwords like *drugs* and *crime*. We are supposed to blink away from that reality. But what happens behind bars, in any country, isn't sealed off from the quality of civil life. "Dehumanization by design" cannot take place behind bars without also occurring in public space at large. In the public spaces of the wealthiest, most powerful of all nations, ours.

Against a background and foreground of crisis, of technology dazzling in means and maniacally violent in substance, among declarations of resignation and predictions of social chaos, I have from time to time—I know I'm not alone in this—felt almost unbearable foreboding, a terrifying loss of gravity, and furious grief. I'm a writer in a country where native-born fascistic tendencies, allied to the practices of "free" marketing, have been trying to eviscerate language of meaning. I have often felt doubly cut off: that I cannot effectively be heard, and that those voices I need most to hear are being cut off from me. Any writer has necessary questions as to whether her words deserve to stand, whether his are worth reading. But it's also been a question, for me, of feeling that almost everything that has fertilized and sustained my work is in danger. I have known that this is, in fact, the very material I have to work with: it is not "in spite of the times" that I will write, but I will try to write, in both senses, *out of my time.*

(There is a 1973 painting by Dorothea Tanning in which the arm of the woman painter literally breaks through the canvas: we don't see the brush, we see the arm up to the wrist, and the gash in the material. That, viscerally, depicts what it means to me, to try to write *out of one's time.*)

I have stayed connected with activism and with people whose phoenix politics are reborn continually out of the nest charred by hostility and lying. I have talked long with other friends. I have searched for words—my own and those of other writers. I've been drawn to those writers, in so many world locations, who have felt the need to question the very activity their lives had been shaped around: to interrogate the value of the written word in the face of many kinds of danger, enormous human needs. I wasn't looking for easy reassurances but rather for evidence that others, in other societies, also had to struggle with that question.

Whatever her or his social identity, the writer is, by the nature of the act of writing, someone who strives for communication and connection, someone who searches, through language, to keep alive the conversation with what Octavio Paz has called "the lost community." Even if what's written feels like a note thrust into a bottle to be thrown into the sea. The Palestinian poet Mahmoud Darwish writes of the incapacity of poetry to find a linguistic equivalent to conditions such as the 1982 Israeli shelling of Beirut: *We are now not to describe, as much as we are to be described. We're being born totally, or else dying totally.* In his remarkable prose-meditation on that war, he also says, *Yet I want to break into song. . . . I want to find a language that transforms language itself into steel for the spirit—a language to use against these sparkling silver insects, these jets. I want to sing. I want a language that I can lean on and that can lean on me, that asks me to bear witness and that I can ask to bear witness, to what power there is in us to overcome this cosmic isolation.*

Darwish writes from the heart of a military massacre. The Caribbean-Canadian poet Dionne Brand writes from colonial diaspora: *I've had moments when the life of my people has been so overwhelming to bear that poetry seemed useless, and I cannot say that there is any moment when I do not think that now.* Yet finally, she admits, like Darwish: *Poetry is here, just here. Something wrestling with how we live, something dangerous, something honest.*

I've gone back many times to Eduardo Galeano's essay "In Defense of the Word," in which he says:

> **I do not share the attitude of those writers who claim for themselves divine privileges not granted to ordinary mortals, nor of those who beat their breasts and rend their clothes as they clamor for public pardon for having lived a life devoted to serving a useless vocation. Neither so godly, nor so contemptible. . . .**
>
> **The prevailing social order perverts or annihilates the creative capacity of the immense majority of people and reduces the possibility of creation—an age-old response to human anguish and the certainty of death—to its professional exercise by a handful of specialists. How many "specialists" are we in Latin America? For whom do we write, whom do we reach? Where is our real public? (Let us mistrust applause. At times we are congratulated by those who consider us innocuous.)**
>
> **To claim that literature on its own is going to change real-**

ity would be an act of madness or arrogance. It seems to me no less foolish to deny that it can aid in making this change.

Galeano's "defense" was written after his magazine, *Crisis,* was closed down by the Argentine government. As a writer in exile, he has continued to interrogate the place of the written word, of literature, in a political order that forbids literacy and creative expression to so many; that denies the value of literature as a vehicle for social change even as it fears its power. Like Nadine Gordimer in South Africa, he knows that censorship can assume many faces, from the shutting down of magazines and the banning of books by some writers, to the imprisonment and torture of others, to the structural censorship produced by utterly unequal educational opportunities and by restricted access to the means of distribution—both features of North American society that have become more and more pronounced over the past two decades.

I question the "free" market's devotion to freedom of expression. Let's bear in mind that when threats of violence came down against the publication and selling of Salman Rushdie's *Satanic Verses,* the chain bookstores took it off their shelves, while independent booksellers continued to stock it. The various small, independent presses in this country, which have had an integral relationship with the independent booksellers, are walking a difficult and risky edge as costs rise, support funding dwindles, and corporate distribution becomes more monolithic. The survival of a great diversity of books, and of work by writers far less internationally notable than Rushdie, depends on diverse interests having the means to make such books available.

It also means a nonelite but educated audience, a population who are literate, who read and talk to each other, who may be factory workers or bakers or bank tellers or paramedicals or plumbers or computer consultants or farmworkers, whose first language may be Croatian or Tagalog or Spanish or Vietnamese but who are given to critical thinking, who care about art, an intelligentsia beyond intellectual specialists.

I have encountered a bracingly hard self-questioning and self-criticism in politically embattled writers, along with their belief that language can be a vital instrument in combating unreality and lies. I have been grateful for their clarity, whether as to Latin America, South Africa, the Caribbean, North America, or the Middle East, about the systems that abuse and waste the majority of human lives. Overall, there is the conviction—and these are writers of poetry, fiction, travel, fantasy—that the writer's freedom to communicate can't be severed from universal public education and universal public access to the word.

Universal public education has two possible—and contradictory—missions. One is the development of a literate, articulate, and well-informed citizenry so that the democratic process can continue to evolve and the promise of radical equality can be brought closer to realization. The other is the perpetuation of a class system dividing an elite, nominally "gifted" few, tracked from an early age, from a very large underclass essentially to be written off as alienated from language and science, from poetry and politics, from history and hope, an underclass to be funneled—whatever its dreams and hopes—toward low-wage temporary jobs. The second is the direction our society has taken. The results are devastating in terms of the betrayal of a generation of youth. The loss to the whole society is incalculable.

But to take the other direction, to choose an imaginative, highly developed, educational system that would serve all citizens at every age—a vast, shared, public schooling in which each of us felt a stake, as with public roads, there when needed, ready when you choose to use them—this would mean changing almost everything else.

It would mean refusing, categorically, the shallow premises of official pieties and banalities. As Jonathan Kozol writes in a "Memo to President Clinton":

> You have spoken at times of the need to put computers into ghetto schools, to set up zones of enterprise in ghetto neighborhoods, and to crack down more aggressively on crime in ghetto streets. Yet you have never asked the nation to consider whether ghetto schools and the ghetto itself represent abhorrent, morally offensive institutions. Is the ghetto . . . to be accepted as a permanent cancer on the body of American democracy? Is its existence never to be challenged? Is its persistence never to be questioned? Is it the moral agenda of our President to do no more than speak about more comely versions of apartheid, of entrepreneurial segregation . . . ?

Well, but of course, voices are saying, we're now seeing the worst of breakaway capitalism, even one or two millionaires are wondering if things haven't gone far enough. Perhaps the thing can be restructured, reinvented? After all, it's all we've got, the only system we in this country have ever known! Without capitalism's lure of high stakes and risk, its glamour of individual power, how could we have conceived, designed, developed the astonishing technological fireworks of the end of this century—this technology with the power to generate ever more swiftly obsolescent products for consumption, ever more wondrous connections among the well connected?

Other voices speak of a technology that can redeem or rescue us. Some who are part of this pyrotechnic moment see it as illuminating enormous possibilities—in education, for one instance. Yet how will this come about without consistent mentoring and monitoring by nontechnical, nonprofit-oriented interests? And where will such mentoring come from? whose power will validate it?

Is technology, rather than democracy, our destiny? Who, what groups, give it direction and purpose? To whom does it really belong? What should be its content? With spectacular advances in medical technology, why not free universal health care? If computers in every ghetto school, why ghettos at all? and why not classroom teachers who are well trained and well paid? If national defense is the issue, why not, as poet-activist Frances Payne Adler suggests, a "national defense" budget that defends the people through affordable health, education, and shelter for everyone? *Why should such minimal social needs be so threatening?* Technology—magnificent, but merely a means after all—will not of itself resolve questions like these.

We need to begin changing the questions. To become less afraid to ask the still-unanswered questions posed by Marxism, socialism and communism. Not to interrogate old, corrupt hierarchical systems, but to ask anew, for our own time: What constitutes ownership? What is work? How can people be assured of a just share in the products of their precious human exertions? How can we move from a production system in which human labor is merely a disposable means to a process that depends on and expands connective relationships, mutual respect, the dignity of work, the fullest possible development of the human subject? How much inequality will we go on tolerating in the world's richest and most powerful nation? What, anyway, is social wealth? Is it only to be defined as private ownership? What does the much abused and trampled word *revolution* mean to us? How can revolutions be prevented from locking in on themselves? how can women and men together imagine "revolution in permanence," continually unfolding through time?

And if we are writers writing first of all from our own desire and need, if this is irresistible work for us, if in writing we experience certain kinds of power and freedom that may be unavailable to us in other ways—surely it would follow that we would want to make that kind of forming, shaping, naming, telling, accessible for anyone who can use it. It would seem only natural for writers to care passionately about literacy, public education, public libraries, public opportunities in all the arts. But more: if we care about the freedom of the word, about language as a liberatory current, if we care about the imagination, we will care about economic justice.

For the pull and suck of Capital's project tend toward reducing, not expanding, overall human intelligence, wit, expressiveness, creative rebellion. If free enterprise is to be totalizingly free, a value in and for itself, it can have no stake in other realms of value. It may pay lip service to charitable works, but its drive is toward what works for the accumulation of wealth; this is a monomaniacal system. Certainly it cannot enrich the realm of the social imagination, least of all the imagination of solidarity and cooperative human endeavor, the unfulfilled imagination of radical equality.

In a poem written in the early 1970s in Argentina, just as the political ground was shifting to a right-wing consolidation, military government, torture, disappearances and massacres, the poet Juan Gelman reflects on delusions of political compromise. The poem is called "Clarities":

> **who has seen the dove marry the hawk**
> **mistrust affection the exploited the exploiter? false**
> **are such unspeakable marriages**
> **disasters are born of such marriages discord sadness**
>
> **how long can the house of such a marriage last?**
> **wouldn't**

> the least breeze grind it down destroy it the sky crush it
> to ruins? oh, my country!
>
> sad! enraged! beautiful! oh my country facing the firing
> squad!
> stained with revolutionary blood!
>
> the parrots the color of mitre
> that go clucking in almost every tree
> and courting on every branch
> are they more alone? less alone? lonely? for
>
> who has seen the butcher marry the tender calf
> tenderness marry capitalism? false
> are such unspeakable marriages
> disasters are born of such marriages discord sadness
> clarities such as
>
> the day itself spinning in the iron cupola
> above this poem

I have talked at some length about capitalism's drive to dis-
enfranchise and dehumanize, to invade the very zones of feeling and relationship we deal with as writers—which Marx
described long ago—because those processes still need to be
described as doing what they still do. I have spoken from the
perspective of a writer and a longtime teacher, trying to grasp
the ill winds and the sharp veerings of her time—a human
being who thinks of herself as an artist, and then must ask herself what that means.

I want to end by saying this to you: We're not simply trapped
in the present. We are not caged within a narrowing corridor
at "the end of history." Nor do any of us have to windsurf on
the currents of a system that depends on the betrayal of so

many others. We do have choices. We're living through a certain part of history that needs us to live it and make it and write it. We can make that history with many others, people we will never know. Or, we can live in default, under protest perhaps, but neutered in our senses and in our sympathies.

We have to keep on asking the questions still being defined as nonquestions—the ones beginning *Why . . . ? What if . . . ?* We will be told these are childish, naive, "pre-postmodern" questions. They are the imagination's questions.

Many of you in this audience are professional intellectuals, or studying to become so, or are otherwise engaged in the activities of a public university. Writers and intellectuals can name, we can describe, we can depict, we can witness—without sacrificing craft, nuance, or beauty. Above all, and at our best, we may sometimes help question the questions.

Let us try to do this, if we do it, without grandiosity. Let's recognize too, without false humility, the limits of the zone in which we work. Writing and teaching are kinds of work, and the relative creative freedom of the writer or teacher depends on the conditions of human labor overall and everywhere.

For what are we, anyway, at our best, but one small, persistent cluster in a greater ferment of human activity—still and forever turning toward, tuned for, the possible, the unrealized and irrepressible design?

1997

Notes

Foreword

Page 2: " 'Thus . . . the sense of having.' " Karl Marx, *Karl Marx: Selected Writings,* ed. David McLellan (New York: Oxford University Press, 1977), pp. 90–92.

Page 3: " 'Now the very idea of the serious. . . .' " Susan Sontag, "Thirty Years Later," *Threepenny Review* (Summer 1996): 6.

Page 4: " 'I am not a marxist.' " See Raya Dunayevskaya, *Rosa Luxemburg, Women's Liberation, and Marx's Philosophy of Revolution,* 2d ed. (Urbana: University of Illinois Press, 1991), p. 105: " 'The world historic defeat of the female sex,' which Engels grounds in a transition from matriarchy (or at least matrilineal descent) to patriarchy, *is no expression of Marx's.* Marx rejected biologism whether in Morgan, Darwin or those Marxists from whom Marx felt it necessary to separate himself so sharply that he used the expression: If that is Marxism, 'I am no Marxist.' " See also Maximilien Rubel and Margaret Manale, *Marx without Myth: A Chronological Study of His Life and Work* (New York: Harper & Row, 1975), and Eugene Kamenka, ed., *The Portable Karl Marx* (New York: Viking, 1983), p. xlv.

Page 8: " 'Language is the presence. . . .' " Karl Marx, *Grundrisse: Foundations of the Critique of Political Economy,* trans. Martin Nicolaus (London: Penguin/New Left Review, 1993), p. 490: "Language as the product of an individual is an impossibility. But the same holds for property. Language itself is the product of a community, just as it is in another respect . . . the presence of the community."

Page 8: " 'The community and its poetry are not two.' " Gary Snyder, *The Real Work: Interviews and Talks, 1964–1979* (New York: New Directions, 1980), p. 174.

"When We Dead Awaken": Writing as Re-Vision

Page 10: " '[Ibsen] shows us that no degradation. . . .' " G. B. Shaw, *The Quintessence of Ibsenism* (New York: Hill & Wang, 1922), p. 139.

Page 12: "By the by, about 'Women,' . . .' " J. G. Stewart, *Jane Ellen Harrison: A Portrait from Letters* (London: Merlin, 1959), p. 140.

Page 13: " 'he once opened his eyes. . . .' " Henry James, "Notes on Novelists," in *Selected Literary Criticism of Henry James,* ed. Morris Shapira (London: Heinemann, 1963), pp. 157–158.

Page 14: "Virginia Woolf is addressing an audience. . . ." In a letter to the composer Ethel Smyth dated June 8, 1933, Woolf speaks of having kept her own personality out of *A Room of One's Own* lest she not be taken seriously: "How personal, so will they say, rubbing their hands with glee, women always are; I even hear them as I write." Henry W. and Albert A. Berg Collection, The New York Public Library, Astor, Lenox and Tilden Foundations.

Page 17: "What I chiefly learned from them was craft." Yet I spent months, at sixteen, memorizing and writing imitations of Millay's sonnets; and in notebooks of that period I find what are obviously attempts to imitate Dickinson's metrics and verbal compression. I knew H.D. only through anthologized lyrics; her epic poetry was not then available to me.

Page 27: "Much of women's poetry. . . ." Was I wholly unaware of the women's blues tradition and its transformation of pain into female agency?

Page 28: "A new generation of women poets. . . ." See Mary Daly, *Beyond God the Father: Toward a Philosophy of Women's Liberation* (Boston: Beacon, 1973).

Blood, Bread, and Poetry: The Location of the Poet

Page 45: ". . . what the critic Edward Said has termed. . . ." Edward Said, "Literature as Values," *New York Times Book Review,* September 4, 1983, 9.

Page 58: " 'Things move so much around you. . . .' " Nancy Morejón, "Elogia de la Dialéctica," in *Breaking the Silences: Twentieth Century Poetry by Cuban Women,* ed. Margaret Randall (Vancouver: Pulp Press, 1982), p. 149.

Page 59: " 'There is the cab driver root and elevator. . . .' " Anita Valerio, "I Am Listening; A Lyric of Roots," in *A Gathering of Spirit: A Collection by North American Indian Women,* ed. Beth Brant (Ithaca, N.Y.: Firebrand Books, 1988), p. 229.

Notes toward a Politics of Location

Page 62: " 'sexuality, politics, . . . work, . . . intimacy. . . .' " See Adrienne Rich, *Of Woman Born: Motherhood as Experience and Institution* (New York: Norton, 1976; 10th ann. ed., 1986), p. 286.

Page 64: " 'the first premise of all human history.' " Karl Marx and Frederick Engels, *The German Ideology,* ed. C. J. Arthur (New York: International Publishers, 1970), p. 42.

Page 65: " 'A female-led peasant rebellion'?" Barbara Ehrenreich and Deirdre English, *Witches, Midwives and Nurses: A History of Women Healers* (Old Westbury, N.Y.: Feminist Press, 1973). See also Ehrenreich and English, *For Her Own Good: 150 Years of the Experts' Advice to Women* (Garden City, N.Y.: Anchor/Doubleday, 1978), pp. 29–37.

Page 68: "*Much of what is narrowly termed 'politics'. . . .*" See Rich, "Women and Honor," above, p. 39.

Page 69: "*The power men everywhere wield over women. . . .*" Adrienne Rich, "Compulsory Heterosexuality and Lesbian Existence" in *Blood, Bread, and Poetry: Selected Prose* (New York: Norton, 1986), p. 68.

Page 70: "the 1977 Combahee River Collective statement. . . ." Barbara Smith, ed., *Home Girls: A Black Feminist Anthology* (New York: Kitchen Table/Women of Color Press, 1983), pp. 272–283. First published in Zillah R. Eisenstein, ed., *Capitalist Patriarchy and the Case for Socialist Feminism* (New York and London: Monthly Review Press, 1978), pp. 362–373.

Page 70: "*To come to terms with the circumscribing nature. . . .*" Gloria I. Joseph, "The Incompatible Ménage à Trois: Marxism, Feminism and Racism," in

Women and Revolution: A Discussion of the Unhappy Marriage of Marxism and Feminism, ed. Lydia Sargent (Boston: South End Press, 1981).

Page 71: "the woman-seeing eye. . . ." See Marilyn Frye, *The Politics of Reality: Essays in Feminist Theory* (Trumansburg, N.Y.: Crossing Press, 1983), p. 171.

Page 72: "the 'deadly sameness' of abstraction." Lillian Smith, "Autobiography as a Dialogue between King and Corpse," in *The Winner Names the Age: A Collection of Writings by Lillian Smith,* ed. Michelle Cliff (New York: Norton, 1978), p. 189.

Page 73: "the overall burying and distortion. . . ." See Elly Bulkin, "Hard Ground: Jewish Identity, Racism, and Anti-Semitism," in Elly Bulkin, Minnie Bruce Pratt, and Barbara Smith, *Yours in Struggle: Three Feminist Perspectives on Anti-Semitism and Racism* (Brooklyn, N.Y.: Long Haul, 1984; distributed by Firebrand Books, Ithaca, N.Y.).

Page 73: "The first American woman astronaut. . . ." See *Ms.,* January 1984, 86.

Page 75: "*The difficulty of saying I.*" Christa Wolf, *The Quest for Christa T.,* trans. Christopher Middleton (New York: Farrar, Straus & Giroux, 1970), p. 174. See also Bernice Reagon, "Turning the Century," in Barbara Smith, pp. 356–368, and Bulkin, pp. 103, 190–193.

Page 76: "*An approach which traces militarism. . . .*" Cynthia Enloe, *Does Khaki Become You?: The Militarisation of Women's Lives* (London: Pluto Press, 1983), ch. 8.

Page 77: " '*A movement helps you to overcome. . . .*' " Sheila Rowbotham, Lynne Segal, and Hilary Wainwright, *Beyond the Fragments: Feminism and the Making of Socialism* (Boston: Alyson, 1981), pp. 55–56.

Page 79: "When I learn that in 1913. . . ." *Women under Apartheid* (London: International Defence and Aid Fund for Southern Africa in co-operation with the United Nations Centre Against Apartheid, 1981), pp. 87–99; Leonard Thompson and Andrew Prior, *South African Politics* (New Haven, Conn.: Yale University Press, 1982). An article in *Sechaba* (published by the African National Congress of South Africa) refers to "the rich tradition of organization and mobilization by women" in the black South African struggle (October 1984), 9.

Page 79: "When I read that a major strand. . . ." Helen Wheatley, "Palestinian

Women in Lebanon: Targets of Repression," *TWANAS: Third World Student Newspaper*, University of California, Santa Cruz (March 1984).

Page 80: " 'She was also subject to another great delusion. . . .' " Etel Adnan, *Sitt Marie Rose*, trans. Georgina Kleege (Sausalito, Calif.: Post-Apollo Press, 1982), p. 101.

Page 81: " 'Women invest hours in cleaning. . . .' " Blanca Figueroa and Jeanine Anderson, "Women in Peru," *International Reports: Women and Society* (1981). See also Ximena Bunster and Elsa M. Chaney, *Sellers and Servants: Working Women in Lima, Peru* (New York: Praeger, 1985), and Madhu Kishwar and Ruth Vanita, *In Search of Answers: Indian Women's Voices from Manushi* (London: Zed, 1984), pp. 56–57.

Page 82: "*This Bridge Called My Back. . . .*" Cherríe Moraga and Gloria Anzaldúa, eds., *This Bridge Called My Back: Writings by Radical Women of Color* (Watertown, Mass.: Persephone, 1981; 2d ed., Albany, N.Y.: Kitchen Table/Women of Color Press, 1984).

Raya Dunayevskaya's Marx

Page 83: " 'I come from Russia 1917. . . .' " Raya Dunayevskaya Archives, microfilm no. 5818, published in *News and Letters*, July 25, 1987, p. 11.

Page 84: " 'the creation of a new society.' " Raya Dunayevskaya, *Women's Liberation and the Dialectics of Revolution* (1985; Detroit: Wayne State University Press, 1996), p. 228.

Page 87: " 'but *from within the left itself.*' " Raya Dunayevskaya, *Rosa Luxemburg, Women's Liberation, and Marx's Philosophy of Revolution* (New Jersey: Humanities Press, 1982), p. 99.

Page 90: " 'the official Moscow publication. . . .' " Raya Dunayevskaya, *Marxism and Freedom from 1776 until Today* (1958; New Jersey: Humanities Press, 1982), pp. 17, 22.

Page 90: "Where Marx had seen. . . ." Dunayevskaya, *Rosa Luxemburg*, pp. 150, 47.

Page 91: " 'a reluctant feminist . . . male chauvinism." *Ibid.*, pp. 85, 27.

Page 91: " 'the poisonous bitch. . . .' " *Ibid.*, p. 27.

Page 91: " 'as independent Marxist revolutionaries,' " *Ibid.*, p. 13.

Page 91: " 'Just imagine, I have become a feminist!' " *Ibid.*, p. 95.

Page 93: " 'in each age, he becomes more alive. . . .' " Dunayevskaya, *Women's Liberation*, p. 174.

Page 93: " 'without a philosophy of revolution. . . .' " Dunayevskaya, *Rosa Luxemburg*, p. 194.

Page 94: " 'the elements of oppression in general. . . .' " *Ibid.*, pp. 180–181.

Page 94: " 'the world historic defeat of the female sex.' " Friedrich Engels, *The Origin of the Family, Private Property, and the State* (New York: International Publishers, 1972), p. 50.

Page 94: " 'to see the possibility of new human relations. . . .' " Dunayevskaya, *Women's Liberation*, p. 202.

Page 96: " 'joyfully [threw her] whole life. . . .' " Dunayevskaya, *Rosa Luxemburg*, p. v.

Page 96: " 'It is from there, in the depths of being. . . .' " Nadine Gordimer, *The Essential Gesture: Writing, Politics and Places* (New York: Knopf, 1988), p. 277.

Page 96: " 'It isn't because we are any "smarter". . . .' " Dunayevskaya, *Rosa Luxemburg*, p. 195.

Page 96: " 'What does being a thinking subject. . . .' " Gloria Anzaldúa, "Haciendo caras, una entrada," in *Making Face, Making Soul / Haciendo Caras: Creative and Critical Perspectives by Feminists of Color,* ed. Gloria Anzaldúa (San Francisco: Spinsters/Aunt Lute, 1990), pp. xxv–xxvi.

Why I Refused the National Medal for the Arts

Page 102: " 'poetry . . . an intolerable hunger.' " Muriel Rukeyser, *The Life of Poetry* (1949; Williamsburg, Mass.: Paris Press, 1996), p. 159.

Page 102: " 'the desire . . . a more profound and ensouled world.' " Clayton Eshleman, *Antiphonal Swing: Selected Prose 1962–1987* (Kingston, N.Y.: McPherson, 1989), p. 136.

Page 103: "For a recent document on this. . . ." Phyllis Kornfeld, *Cellblock Visions: Prison Art in America* (Princeton: Princeton University Press, 1997).

Page 104: " 'Due process asks . . . of human nature and experience.' " *New York Times,* July 25, 1997, C19.

Poetry and the Public Sphere

Page 115: "Recently, I read an essay by Charles Bernstein. . . ." Charles Bernstein, *A Poetics* (Cambridge, Mass.: Harvard University Press, 1992), pp. 4–5.

Page 118: " 'cling to / what we've grasped too well.' " *Ibid.*, p. 89.

Page 118: "to 'intensify / our relationships.' " *Ibid.*, p. 88.

Muriel Rukeyser: Her Vision

Page 121: "The critic Louise Kertesz. . . ." Louise Kertesz, *The Poetic Vision of Muriel Rukeyser* (Baton Rouge: Louisiana State University Press, 1980), pp. 78–84.

Page 121: " 'The city rises in its light. . . ." Muriel Rukeyser, *The Life of Poetry* (1949; Williamsburg, Mass.: Paris Press, 1996), p. 192.

Page 121: " 'except in the servants' rooms. . . .' " *Ibid.*, p. 197.

Page 122: " 'I was expected to grow up. . . .' " Janet Sternburg, ed., *The Writer on Her Work,* I (New York: Norton, 1980), p. 221.

Page 122: "the Scottsboro case." Nine African American youths were unjustly convicted of raping two white women, a conviction later overturned by the Supreme Court, and a landmark issue for radicals.

Page 124: " 'My themes and the use I have made of them. . . .' " Muriel Rukeyser, "Poet . . . Woman . . . American . . . Jew," *Contemporary Jewish Record* 5, no. 7 (February 1944); repr. *Bridges: A Journal for Jewish Feminists and Our Friends* 1, no. 1 (Spring 1990): 23–29.

Page 127: "It's to be hoped. . . ." Paris Press in Williamsburg, Massachusetts, has reprinted *The Life of Poetry,* with a foreword by Jane Cooper (1996), and *The Orgy* (1965), her biomythographical novel, with a foreword by Sharon Olds (1997).

Arts of the Possible

Page 152: "the Combahee River Collective statement." Barbara Smith, ed., *Home Girls: A Black Feminist Anthology* (New York: Kitchen Table/Women of Color Press, 1983), pp. 272–283. See also Zillah R. Eisenstein, ed., *Capital-*

ist Patriarchy and the Case for Socialist Feminism (New York: Monthly Review Press, 1978).

Page 153: " 'a visionary relation to reality.' " Aijaz Ahmad, *In Theory: Classes, Nations, Literatures* (New York and London: Verso, 1992), p. 154.

Page 154: "They have also been disparaged. . . ." *Ibid.,* pp. 4–5, 129.

Page 155: " 'For a writer, as you live. . . .' " Garrett Hongo, ed., *Under Western Eyes: Personal Essays from Asian America* (New York: Anchor, 1995), pp. 23–24.

Page 156: "In place of all the physical and spiritual senses. . . ." Karl Marx, as quoted by Raya Dunayevskaya, *Women's Liberation and the Dialectics of Revolution* (1985; Detroit: Wayne State University Press, 1996), p. 25. See also Karl Marx, *Karl Marx: Selected Writings,* ed. David McLellan (New York: Oxford University Press, 1977), p. 92.

Page 158: " 'the barest illusion of rehabilitation. . . .' " Mumia Abu-Jamal, *Live from Death Row* (New York: Addison-Wesley, 1995), pp. 89–90.

Page 159: " 'We are now not to describe. . . .' " Mahmoud Darwish, *Memory for Forgetfulness: August, Beirut, 1982* (Berkeley: University of California Press, 1995), pp. 65, 52.

Page 160: " 'I've had moments when the life of my people. . . .' " Dionne Brand, *Bread Out of Stone: Recollections, Sex, Recognitions, Race, Dreaming, Politics* (Toronto: Coach House Press, 1994), pp. 182–183.

Page 160: "I've gone back many times. . . ." Eduardo Galeano, *Days and Nights of Love and War,* trans. Judith Brister (New York: Monthly Review Press, 1983), pp. 191, 185, 192.

Page 163: "As Jonathan Kozol writes. . . ." Jonathan Kozol, "Two Nations, Eternally Unequal," in *Tikkun* 12, no. 1 (1996): 14.

Page 165: " 'who has seen the dove marry the hawk. . . .' " Juan Gelman, *Unthinkable Tenderness: Selected Poems,* ed. and trans. Joan Lindgren (Berkeley: University of California Press, 1997), p. 12.

Acknowledgments

Declaration of thanks:

—to Michelle Cliff,
closest and most demanding interlocutor
from her archipelago of language

—to Suzanne Gardinier,
whose belief and critiques have made this
a stronger book

—to Frances Goldin,
for keeping the faith and acting on it

—to Steven Barclay,
for comradeship beyond the call

—to the Lannan Foundation,
for manifold vision and generosity

Index

abstraction, 65–67, 72
Abu-Jamal, Mumia, 158
Accumulation of Capital
　(Luxemburg), 90
Achterberg, Gerrit, 133
Adler, Frances Payne, 164
Adler, Viktor, 91
Adnan, Etel, 80
affirmative action, 117
African Americans, 5–6, 50, 51,
　67, 130
　civil rights movement of, 54,
　　73, 89
　Dunayevskaya and, 83, 84, 86,
　　88–89
　feminism of, 70, 81–82
　"identity politics" and, 152–53
　Marx and, 86, 88
　in prison, 157–58
　see also race
Ahmad, Aijaz, 133, 154
Aidoo, Ama Ata, 61
Alexander, Jane, 98–99
Alexander, Meena, 115
alienation, 2, 8, 41, 59, 109, 112
Altieri, Charles, 128–31
American Indians, 59–60, 94,
　148

American Poets in 1976 (Heyen,
　ed.), 10
amnesia, lying and, 32
anticommunism, 4, 49, 52–53,
　72, 73, 140
anti-Marxism, 3–4, 39, 69
anti-Semitism, 45, 78, 91, 109
　Holocaust and, 42, 143
Anzaldúa, Gloria, 96–97
apartheid:
　of literary culture, 109–11
　in South Africa, 79
Arabs, 144
arts:
　education and, 101, 103
　fear and hatred of, 52–53, 104
　federal funding for, 99–101,
　　104–5
　as higher world view, 44–45,
　　52
　lack of thought about, 112
　politics and, 41–42, 46–61
　social presence of, 99, 102–5
　see also specific topics
"Arts of the Possible" (Rich),
　146–67, 175n-76n
Asia Society, 133
astronauts, female, 73–74

Atlas of the Difficult World, An
  (Rich), 139
"Atlas of the Difficult World, An"
  (Rich), 141–42
"Aunt Jennifer's Tigers" (Rich),
  17
Austen, Jane, 14, 28

"Backside of the Academy, The"
  (Rukeyser), 123
Baldwin, James, 50, 51, 55, 56,
  61
Bambara, Toni Cade, 61
Beauvoir, Simone de, 50, 51, 55,
  92
Bebel, August, 91
Berger, John, 107
Berman, Sandra, 128, 132–34
Bernstein, Charles, 112–15, 117,
  118, 128
Best American Poetry 1996 (Rich,
  ed.), 106–14
Bishop, Elizabeth, 13
blacks, *see* African Americans
Blake, William, 44, 46
Blaser, Robin, 137
"Blood, Bread, and Poetry"
  (Rich), 41–61, 170*n*–71*n*
body, 64–65
  politics of location in, 64–68
  truth of, 34, 35
Brand, Dionne, 61, 160
Breaking the Silences (Randall,
  ed.), 58
Brennan, William, 103–4
Bridges, 144
Brooks, Gwendolyn, 92
Browning, Elizabeth Barrett, 48
Burger's Daughter (Gordimer), 96
Burlak, Anne, 125

Byron, George Gordon, Lord,
  46

California, Proposition 209 in,
  117
*Cambridge Book of Poetry for
  Children, The,* 44
Capital (Marx), 88
capitalism, 2, 4, 5, 11, 37, 139,
  147–49, 163
  Marx's depiction of, 4, 90, 94,
  95, 156
  women's liberation and, 56,
  57, 116
Cellblock Visions (Kornfeld), 103
censorship, 6, 161
Central America, 72
  see also Nicaragua
Césaire, Aimé, 102
Char, René, 132, 141
China, People's Republic of, 148
City College, New York, 55
civilization, Marx's views on, 94
civil rights movement, 54, 73,
  89
"Clarities" (Gelman), 165–66
class, 11, 70, 90, 95, 162
  gender vs., 4, 5, 86
  intersection of race and, 5, 6,
  70
Clinton, Bill, 98–100
Cold War, 45, 49, 51, 72–73
Coleman, Wanda, 113
colonialism, 2, 51, 74, 94
Combahee River Collective, 70,
  81, 152
commodity culture, 2–3, 74,
  149–50, 156
  art vs., 7, 59
  poetry and, 7, 111–12, 116

communism, 72, 147–48, 164
  primitive, 94
  see also anticommunism; Cold
    War; Soviet Union
Communist party, Soviet, 88
Communist party, U.S., 73, 85
community:
  language and, 8, 169*n*
  "lost," 159
  poetry and, 8, 115–16
"Compulsory Heterosexuality and
  Lesbian Existence" (Rich),
  69
Congress, U.S., 101, 156
consciousness:
  awakening of, 10–11, 27
  "false," 154
  language and images for, 12,
    134
  male, 28, 29
conversation, 161–62
  democracy and, 117
  lack of, 19–20
Creeley, Robert, 136, 137
Crisis, 161
Cuban women poets, 58, 71

Dahlen, Beverly, 135–36
Daly, Mary, 28
Dark Fields of the Republic
  (Rich), 139, 140
Darwish, Mahmoud, 159–60
"Defying the Space That
  Separates" (Rich), 106–14
democracy, 9, 72, 107, 164
  art and, 103
  conversation and, 117
  education and, 162
  as free enterprise, 147
Democratic party, U.S., 100

Derricotte, Toi, 129
destiny, white delusion of, 57
de Vries, Hendrik, 133
Díaz-Diocaretz, Myriam, 62
Dickinson, Emily, 16, 170*n*
Di Prima, Diane, 129
disenfranchised, artists'
  connections with, 130–31
domesticity, 19–21, 34, 45
*Dream of a Common Language,
  The* (Rich), 129
Dropkin, Celia, 133
Du Bois, W. E. B., 82
due process, 104
Dunayevskaya, Raya, 6–7,
  83–97, 173*n*–74*n*
Duncan, Robert, 136–37
DuPlessis, Rachel Blau, 115,
  135–36
Dutch poetry, 133

Eastern Europe, 46, 51, 88, 104,
  148
East German workers' strike
  (1953), 88
education, 161–63
  in arts, 101, 103
  political, of students, 154
election of 1980, 140
Emmens, Jan, 133
Engels, Friedrich, 87, 92, 93, 94,
  169*n*
England, 57, 77–78, 140
English, Black vs. Standard, 55
"Eros Turannos" (Robinson), 44
Eshleman, Clayton, 102
ethical responsibility, 3, 141–42
Ethnological Notebooks (Marx),
  92, 93–94
existentialism, 51

"experimental" ("innovative")
writing, 113, 114, 135–36

fantasy vs. imagination, 20–21
FBI (Federal Bureau of
Investigation), 45, 53
fear:
of art, 52–53, 104
lying and, 32, 36–37, 38
in McCarthy era, 53
feminism, *see* women's liberation
movement
Fraser, Kathleen, 135–36
freedom, 21, 43, 51, 72, 73, 97
capitalism and, 147, 148
of expression, 161
French poetry, 132
Friedman, Susan Stanford, 115

Galeano, Eduardo, 160–61
Gathering of Spirit, A (anthology
of North American Indian
women), 59–60
Gelman, Juan, 165–66
gender, 139
class vs., 4, 5, 86
intersection of race, class, and,
5
Marx's interest in, 94
race vs., 5, 70, 86
see also women's liberation
movement
gender differences, poetry and,
128–30
genocide, against tribal peoples,
148, 149
Germany, Weimar Republic of,
140
Ghalib, Mirza, 133
Gibbs, Willard, 125

Gide, André, 51
Ginsberg, Allen, 136, 137
Giscombe, C. S., 113
Golden Treasury, The (Palgrave),
44
Gonne, Maud, 16
Gordimer, Nadine, 96, 161
Grahn, Judy, 61, 129, 135–36
Greenberg, Eliezer, 133
Guild Complex, 111

Hahn, Kimiko, 113
"Halfway" (Rich), 20
Hamer, Fannie Lou, 82
Hansberry, Lorraine, 82, 100, 101
"Harpers Ferry" (Rich), 138
Harrison, Jane, 12, 13
Harvard University, 46–47
H. D. (Hilda Doolittle), 16, 48,
170*n*
Hegel, G. W. F., 85, 87
Heresies, 30
Herschel, Caroline, 25
Herschel, William, 25
"Her Vision" (Rich), 6
Herzberg, Judith, 133
heterosexuality, 36, 56
Heyen, William, 10
history, 49–51, 166–67
double, 107
Jewish view of, 142–43
Hitler, Adolf, 72, 140
Holocaust, 42, 143
homosexuality, 45
see also lesbians
Hongo, Garrett, 155
honor, honorable life, 30–36
difficulties in construction of,
3, 38–40
female, 31, 33, 35

male idea of, 30–31
  politicians' lack of, 31
House Un-American Activities
  Committee, 101
Howe, Irving, 133
Howe, Susan, 135–36
(How)ever, 135–36
Hughes, Langston, 48
humanism, of Marx, 7, 86, 90,
  93
Hungarian Revolution (1956),
  88

Ibsen, Henrik, 2, 10
identity(ies), 11, 50
  American, 75
  fragmented, 49, 60, 138
  gender, 135
  sexual, 6, 11
  white, 67, 109, 110
  of writer, 159
"identity politics," 152–53
illiteracy, 60
images:
  race and, 109
  of Sisyphus, 6
  spiritual power of, 78–79
imagination:
  apartheid of, 111
  art and, 103
  autobiographical elements vs.,
    138
  fantasy vs., 20–21
  oppositional, 8
  subversive function of, 21
imperialism, 46, 54, 57, 90
incarceration, 147, 157–58
"In Defense of the Word"
  (Galeano), 160–61
India, 148

Indians, American, 59–60, 94,
  148
"Inscriptions" (Rich), 136, 139
isolation, 19–20, 28, 33, 51

James, C. L. R., 82
James, Henry, 13
Jewish Quarterly, 138
Jews, 42, 45, 64, 68, 78, 124
  history and, 142–43
  see also anti-Semitism
Jews Against Genocide, 144
Jews for Racial and Economic
  Justice, 144
Jogiches, Leo, 95
Jordan, June, 82, 111, 117, 119
Joseph, Gloria I., 82
Just above My Head (Baldwin),
  61
justice, 3, 5, 6, 9, 72

Kahlo, Frida, 61
Kautsky, Louise, 91
Keats, John, 46
Kertesz, Louise, 121
Khalife, Iman, 79–80
Khrushchev Report, 73
King, Martin Luther, Jr., 6
"Kingfishers, The" (Olson), 136
Korn, Rachel, 133
Kornfeld, Phyllis, 103
Kozol, Jonathan, 163

language, 6, 16
  common, 113, 134–35
  community and, 8, 169n
  of consciousness, 12, 134
  degradation of, 7–8, 72, 107,
    114, 116–17, 147, 149,
    158–59

language (*continued*)
  historical roots of, 72
  liberation vs. entrapment by,
    11
  poetic, 7–8, 108, 109, 113–14,
    116–19
  poetry as exploration of, 116
  politics of, 55
  public, disruption of, 7
  of Woolf, 14, 170*n*
Latin American poetry, 133
Lawrence, Jacob, 61
"Leaflets" (Rich), 136, 137
Leaves of Hypnos (Char), 132
Lebanon, 79–80, 159–60
Ledbetter, James, 110
Lehman, David, 106
Lei-Lanilau, Carolyn, 113
Lenin, V. I., 87, 88
Lerner, Gerda, 92
lesbians, 36, 45, 55, 64
LeSueur, Meridel, 53
Levertov, Denise, 136
Levi, Jan Heller, 120
Lévi-Strauss, Claude, 69
Life of Poetry, The (Rukeyser),
    126
literacy, 130, 161–62
literature:
  apartheid in, 109–11
  autobiographical elements vs.
    imagination in, 138
  radical critique of, 11–12
  see also specific topics
"Living in the Interregnum"
    (Gordimer), 96
*London Times Literary
    Supplement*, 123
"Long Conversation, A" (Rich),
    136, 139, 141

Lorde, Audre, 61, 82, 92, 111,
    129
"Loser, The" (Rich), 18–19
Lubbock, John, 93
Luxemburg, Rosa, 90–92, 95–96

McCarthyism, 52–53, 73
Maine, Henry, 93
Malcolm X, 6, 82
male role, for female artist,
    13–14
"Marghanita" (Rich), 138
marriage, 19–21, 34, 44, 49
Marx, Karl, 2–5, 8, 63, 64, 69,
    145, 156, 157, 166
  Dunayevskaya's views on,
    83–97, 173*n*–74*n*
  humanism of, 7, 86, 90, 93
  questions raised by, 102
Marxism, 3–4, 39, 69, 70, 102,
    147–48, 164, 169*n*
Marxism and Freedom
    (Dunayevskaya), 87–89
Massachusetts Review, 146
mass entertainment culture, 7
matriarchy (matrilineal descent),
    94, 169*n*
Matthiessen, Francis Otto,
    45–46, 126
meaning, removed from
    language, 107, 114, 158
"mean-spiritedness," 156–57
media, 3, 7, 59
"Memo to President Clinton"
    (Kozol), 163
Mérimée, Prosper, 13
middle class, 147, 157
  self-absorption of, 3
Middle East, violence in, 78,
    79–80, 159–60

Midnight Salvage (Rich), 132, 134, 139, 141
Millay, Edna St. Vincent, 16, 170*n*
"Miner's Wives, The" (Dunayevskaya), 89
Modern Language Association, 10, 123, 128–37
Modotti, Tina, 141
Molodowsky, Kadya, 133, 143
Montgomery bus boycott, 88, 89
Moore, Marianne, 13, 16, 126
Morejón, Nancy, 61
Morgan, Lewis Henry, 93, 94
Morrison, Toni, 113
multiculturalism, 115
Muriel Rukeyser Reader (Levi, ed.), 120
Murray, Gilbert, 12
music, 131–32
myth, 12, 15–16, 21, 50, 124

naming, act of, 11
Nation, 117
National Endowment for the Arts, 99, 101
national liberation movements, 92
National Medal for the Arts, Rich's refusal of, 98–105, 174*n*
National Writers' Voice Project, 111
Native Women in the Arts, 111
New Deal, art and, 104–5
New Jewish Agenda, 144
Nicaragua, 41–42, 58–59, 61, 71–72
Nielsen, Aldon, 109

"Notes toward a Politics of Location" (Rich), 1, 62–82

Olsen, Tillie, 53
Olson, Charles, 136, 137
Oppen, George, 137
oppositional imagination, 8
origins, obsession with, 78–79
"Origins and History of Consciousness" (Rich), 135
Origins of the Family (Engels), 92, 93
"Orion" (Rich), 23–25
Ostriker, Alicia, 115
Our Sister Killjoy (Aidoo), 61
Owen, Maureen, 135–36
Oxford Book of English Verse, 44

pain:
   communal and public, 114, 149
   lying and, 32, 38
   truth and, 39
Palestinian state, 144
Paris Review, 112
patriarchy, 28–29, 36, 57, 58, 169*n*
   lying and, 34
   as model for other forms of domination, 11, 69–70
Paz, Octavio, 8, 159
Perelman, Bob, 115
personal, the:
   in poetry, 109
   retreat into, 154–55
"personal is political, the," 2, 55
personal narrative:
   as feminist expression, 2
   replacing critical argument, 2–3

Peru, 81
Phear, John Budd, 93, 94
Philosophy and Revolution
(Dunayevskaya), 89–90
"Planetarium" (Rich), 25–27
Plath, Sylvia, 12
"Poem Beginning with a Line by
Pindar, A" (Duncan),
136–37
"Poem out of Childhood"
(Rukeyser), 122
Poetics, A (Bernstein), 112–13
poetics, poetry, 1, 15–29, 41–61,
106–45
avant-garde, 7
commodity culture and, 7,
111–12, 116
complexity and fecundity of,
33
of Cuban women, 58, 71
difference and identity in,
112–13
indestructibility of, 42
language of, 7–8, 108, 109,
113–14, 116–19
maturity in, 114
music of, 131–32
in Nicaragua, 41
out of political experiences,
136
personal, 109
politics and, 28, 41–42,
46–48, 53–55, 58–61, 136
public life and, 115–19,
175*n*
as revelation, 43
Rukeyser's definition of, 124
self-absorption in, 112
translation of, 133–34
about women, by men, 15–16

see also specific poems and
poets
"Poetry and the Public Sphere"
(Rich), 115–19, 175*n*
"Poetry, Feminism(s) and the
Difficult Wor(l)d" (panel),
115, 116
Poetry for the People, 111
politics, politicians, 22
art and, 41–42, 46–61
honor and, 31, 38–39
"identity," 152–53
of language, 55
of location, 57, 62–82,
171*n*–73*n*
lying of, 31
manipulation and, 52
poetry and, 28, 41–42, 46–48,
53–55, 58–61, 136
sexual, 54
women's movement and,
151–52
Pollitt, Katha, 110
poverty, 5, 157
power, 8–9, 50, 115
lying and, 35
male, 11–13, 28
media, 3, 7
racism and, 109
privacy, 19, 35–36, 38, 56
proletariat, female, 74
public life:
commodity culture in control
of, 2–3
poetry and, 115–19, 175*n*
and private life, 55–56
publishing industry, 154–55,
161

Quartermain, Peter, 128, 134–37

race, 2, 8, 50
 class vs., 5, 70
 gender vs., 5, 70, 86
 intersection of class and, 5, 6,
  70
 poetry and, 109–11
 see also African Americans;
  whites
racism, 5, 36, 46, 47, 57, 95, 109
 Baldwin's views on, 51
Randall, Margaret, 58
"Raya Dunayevskaya's Marx"
  (Rich), 4, 83–97, 173n–74n
"Readings of History" (Rich), 142
Reagan, Ronald, 3, 140
Reagon, Bernice, 82
Republican party, U.S., 100
Retallack, Joan, 135–36
re-vision:
 need for, 11–12
 writing as, 10–29
revolution, 41
 avant-garde tradition and, 7
 experience and, 84
 permanent (continuing), 88,
  96, 116
 resistance of women in, 94
 "total," 93
 women's liberation and, 116
Rexroth, Kenneth, 123
Ridge, Lola, 121
Robinson, Edwin Arlington, 44
Room of One's Own, A (Woolf),
  14, 170n
Rosa Luxemburg, Women's
  Liberation and Marx's
  Philosophy of Revolution
  (Dunayevskaya), 83, 85,
  90–92, 93, 95–96
Rossetti, Christina, 16

Rowbotham, Sheila, 77, 92
Rukeyser, Muriel, 48, 102, 108,
  120–27, 175n
 background of, 121–22
 critical assessment of, 123
 as Jew, 124
 as mentor, 6, 123, 126
Rushdie, Salman, 161
Russell, Michele, 82
Russian poetry, 132–33
Russian revolution, 88, 90

Said, Edward, 45
Salt Eaters, The (Bambara), 61
Sand, George, 13
Sandinistas, 59
Sappho, 16, 78
Satanic Verses (Rushdie), 161
science, Rukeyser's view of, 123,
  124, 125
Seidman, Hugh, 137
self-absorption:
 middle class, 3
 in poetry, 112
self-knowledge, 11
sex, sexuality, 13, 22, 55, 56, 139
 lying and, 34, 36
sexual identity, change in concept
  of, 6, 11
Shakespeare, William, 14, 28
Shaw, George Bernard, 10
silence, 150–51
 art as breaker of, 99
 dead, 151
 lying with, 31, 34, 36
 poetry and, 109
 political, 154
 of unconscious, 32
Silver Pennies (anthology), 44
Simone, Nina, 61

Sisyphus, image of, 6
Sitt Marie Rose (Adnan), 80
slavery, slave trade, 88, 94, 101, 148, 149
"Sleepwalking Next to Death" (Rich), 133
Smith, Barbara, 82
Smith, Lillian, 72
Snapshots of a Daughter-in-Law (Rich), 129, 136, 139
"Snapshots of a Daughter-in-Law" (Rich), 23, 141
Snyder, Gary, 8
socialism, 56, 57, 72, 147–48, 164
Socialist Workers party, 89
Sontag, Susan, 3
South Africa, 78, 79, 148
South African Politics (book), 79
Soviet Union, 46, 49, 72, 88
spiritual power of images, 78–79
Stalin, Joseph, 87, 88
Stalinism, 4, 72, 88
Stevens, Wallace, 46, 126
Stewart, Susan, 128, 134
Student Nonviolent Coordinating Committee, 87
suffering, personal or familial, 114
survival:
 lying for, 34–35
 re-vision for, 11, 13

Taggard, Genevieve, 121
Tanenhaus, Beverley, 30
Tanning, Dorothea, 159
technological change, technology, 1, 2, 8, 19, 60, 158, 163–64
Thatcher, Margaret, 140

Theory of Flight (Rukeyser), 122, 126
Third World, 74, 88, 90, 93
This Bridge Called My Back (anthology), 82
Three Guineas (Woolf), 57, 63
Time's Power (Rich), 138
translations, 133–34
Treasury of Yiddish Poetry, A (Howe and Greenberg, eds.), 133
Trotsky, Leon, 87, 92
Trotsky, Natalia, 92
Truth, Sojourner, 82

United States, 62–64
 delusion of destiny in, 57
 double history of, 107
 McCarthy era in, 52–53, 73
 military-"private" sector link in, 74
 politics of location of, 71–72, 74, 75
 radical movements in, 5, 73, 84, 87, 89
Untermeyer, Louis, 44
Urdu poetry, 133

Valerio, Anita, 59–60
van Geel, Chr. J., 133
Vietnam War, 8, 54–55
violence, 6, 50, 63, 78, 148
 in Middle East, 78, 79–80, 159–60
Vroman, Leo, 133

Wakoski, Diane, 12
Watkins, Mary, 61
wealth, 5, 99
 accumulation of, 101, 104

Weimar Republic, 140
welfare, 5
Wells-Barnett, Ida B., 82
West Virginia miners' strike
    (1949–50), 84, 87, 89
What Is Found There (Rich), 7,
    142
When We Dead Awaken (Ibsen),
    2, 10
"When We Dead Awaken" (Rich),
    2, 10–29, 170*n*
"White Night" (Molodowsky),
    133
whites, 49, 57
    identity of, 67, 109, 110
    literary magazines and, 109,
        110
    poetry of, 109
    politics of location and, 70–71,
        74, 77–78, 81–82
"Why I Refused the National
    Medal for the Arts" (Rich),
    98–105, 174*n*
Williams, William Carlos, 126,
    136
Willkie, Wendell, 124
Will to Change, The (Rich), 129,
    136
Wolf, Christa, 75
Wollstonecraft, Mary, 50–51,
    141
Woman Is Talking to Death, A
    (Grahn), 135–36
"Woman Question," Luxemburg's
    views on, 91
woman writers, male judgment
    on, 13–14, 15, 170*n*
women:
    anger of, 13, 14, 27–28, 56, 82
    as luxury, 10, 13

lying of, 31–35
male artist and thinker's use
    of, 10–13, 15–16, 28
in miner's strike, 87, 89
"Women and Honor" (Rich), 3–4,
    30–40
*Women, Feminist Identity and
    Society in the 1980s* (Díaz-
    Diocaretz and Zavala, eds.),
    62
women's culture, 5, 71
*Women's Liberation and the
    Dialectics of Revolution*
    (Dunayevskaya), 83, 87, 89,
    92
women's liberation movement
    (feminism), 1–6, 11, 55–57,
    65, 151–53
    anti-Marxism of, 3–4, 39, 69
    as self-involvement or self-
        improvement, 3
    black, 70, 81–82
    Dunayevskaya and, 84, 86–87,
        89, 91, 92, 93, 95
    Marx and, 86, 93
    personal narrative as
        expression of, 2
    poetry and, 129–30
    politics of location and, 62–82
    radical, 15, 69, 70, 86
    revolution and, 116
    shortcomings of, 5
    sources of, 73, 82
    women's culture vs., 5
Woolf, Virginia, 14–15, 27–28,
    37, 57, 63
Wordsworth, William, 45, 129
Working Class Kitchen, The, 111
Work of a Common Woman, The
    (Grahn), 135–36

writing:
  out of one's time, 159–61
  as re-vision, 10–29
Wylie, Elinor, 16

Yale Younger Poets Prize, 122,
  126
Yeats, William Butler, 46–49

Yiddish poetry, 133
"Yom Kippur 1984" (Rich), 136

Zabielski, Laverne, 111
Zaturenska, Marya, 121
Zavala, Iris, 62
Zetkin, Clara, 91